MANUAL OF GRENADES

AND

NEW GRENADE CHART

German-British-American

Compiled by Major J. I. Cowan

The Naval & Military Press Ltd

Published by

The Naval & Military Press Ltd
Unit 5 Riverside, Brambleside
Bellbrook Industrial Estate
Uckfield, East Sussex
TN22 1QQ England

Tel: +44 (0)1825 749494

www.naval-military-press.com
www.nmarchive.com

In reprinting in facsimile from the original, any imperfections are inevitably reproduced and the quality may fall short of modern type and cartographic standards.

NOTE

✠ **Famous Last Words** ✠ will be seen throughout this book; they are merely to impress upon all users of grenades that when properly handled, grenades will only be dangerous to the enemy. Accidents are invariably caused by sheer carelessness.

Readers should refer to the Summary Chart after having carefully studied the remainder of the book.

I have included some details of the best known American Grenades in this book, as it is quite clear that British and American Forces are, and will be combining, in the various theatres of war. It is therefore, advisable to have some knowledge of the weapons, especially Grenades used by both Forces. I feel therefore, it would be of similar benefit to the U.S. Services to know something about our Grenades for the same reason. If this is achieved even in small measure, I hope this book will have served its purpose.

AUTHOR.

GRENADE

Type.	A. How Recognised when issued.	B. Description.	C. Type of Fuse and Ignition.	D. When, Where and How Grenade should be used.
1 No. 36 Mills Grenade (Hand and Cup Discharger).	Live: Dark Brown, Black in colour, Varnished. Red and/or Green marks round top of body. Practice: Gray-White.	Barrel shaped. Serrated to assist fragmentation on explosion. Weight 1½ lbs.	TIME. .22 Rim Fire Cap. 4-second Fuse, White (Hand-thrown) E.Y. Cup Discharger 7-second Fuse. Buff. Fuse is fitted to detonator. Filled Baratol.	Anti-Personnel. Generally bowled over-arm from cover. For clearing Buildings, Trenches, M.G. Nests, etc. Fired from Discharger Cup at 45 unless in certain types of town fighting. Propellant, Ballistite Cartridge only Recoil considerable. Use shock absorber at butt.
2 No. 36. Fired from Northover with gas check (if E.Y. Cup Discharger not available).	As above—see 1A.	As above—see 1B.	As above—see 1 C. 7-second Fuse, but tests have proved that 4-second Fuse can be used.	As above—see 1 D. Propellant—5 drams Powder. Remove Rubber Shock Pad from Propellant.
3 No. 68. Anti-Tank Rifle Grenade.	Painted Buff, with Red and Green Band round Body. Must not be Stripped. Practice: White.	Tail Unit screws into the Body. Tail Unit has a central Sleeve and Four Vanes. Fixed Gas Check. Weight 1¾ lbs.	Detonates Instantly when head of grenade impacts on solid object. Special H.E. or 6¼-oz. Lyddite.	Fired from Discharger (Ballistite Cartridge only) against all armoured fighting vehicles, lorries, etc. Some forms of Demolition. Propellant 30 grain Ballistite Cartridge, half a length of which for .303 is black. For .300 cartridge has open end crimped. Recoil considerable. Use shock absorber.
4 No. 69. Bakelite Hand Grenade issued complete except for priming. Must not be stripped.	Black Bakelite. Red Band or X's round top of body. Practice: White.	Barrel shape. Similar to 36 M. Weight approximately 1 lb.	"All-ways" percussion. Instantaneous on Impact. Amatol or Lyddite.	Anti - Personnel (Blast). Morale generally. Confined spaces best effects. Useful in dry weather for making dust cloud if smoke not available. Can be thrown any method as situation demands. Can be used under certain conditions as "Aid to Realism" in exercises and battle practice.
5 No. 73. A.T. Grenade.	Painted Buff with Red Band, and Stencilled 73 A.T. Practice: White.	Cylindrical. 10 ins. high, 3 ins. diameter Thermos Flask. Weight 4 lbs. approx.	"All-ways" Instantaneous. Percussion. Gelignite, 3½ lbs. approximately.	Against all Lorries, A.F.Vs., etc. Can also be used in numbers as Mines, etc., in street fighting, with correct Fusing. Above from Buildings. Generally thrown over-arm, held with fingers either side of safety tape.

SUMMARY CHART.

E. Range and Danger Area.	F. Type of Effects.	G. To Prepare and Prime.	H. Mechanism in Operation.
Hand, 25-35 yards. Can inflict wounds up to 100 yards. Cup Discharger, Gas Port fully open, 80 yards at 45°. Gas Port fully closed, 200 yards at 45°.	Anti-Personnel. Fragments in all directions parallel to ground and upwards. Shrapnel effects can be obtained if thrown to burst about 6 feet or more above objective. Ditto Cup Discharger.	Remove Base Plug, clean and examine carefully. Test Spring for tension: if weak reject. Ensure Striker moves freely in sleeve. Insert Igniter Set without using force. Attach Gas Check for use with E.Y. Cup.	Withdrawal of Safety Pin leaves hand (or Cup Discharger) in control of Lever. When Grenade is thrown or fired, Lever flies off and releases striker, which is forced on to the Cap of Igniter Set by the Spring, and Ignites Fuse, which burns for 4-seconds (7-seconds E.Y. Cup), explodes detonator which explodes Grenade. Keep Lever in palm of hand when throwing.
As above—see 1 E. 75-150 yards.	As above—see 1 F. But Shrapnel effects easier to obtain.	As above—see 1 G. But Northover.	As above—see 1 H. But read "Breech" instead of Discharger.
50-100 yards. Special Sight. Gas Port on Discharger fully closed always. Blast concentrated in limited forward area but pieces of tail will fly considerable distances.	Penetration. On. Impact will perforate armour of light, medium, and sometimes parts of heavy Tanks.	Ready for use when issued.	Pull out Safety Pin. Place Grenade, Gas Check end Fins first, into Cup. Shear Wire breaks on firing leaving Striker free. When fired from Northover Shear Wire does not break until target is struck with sufficient force to do this, therefore, only use Northover when Cup Discharger not available.
Generally up to 50 yards. Hand only. Small Radius, approx. 10 yards. For exercises consider 35 yards radius as danger area. In Practice all "Blinds" must be found and destroyed, as will explode if trodden on.	Anti-Personnel. Blast. Lethal under some conditions. Momentary Shock. Morale.	Remove Base Plug. Insert Detonator open end first. Replace Base Plug.	Remove Safety Cap, Safety Tape being held in position by thumb and finger of throwing hand. When thrown, Safety Bolt on Tape falls out. Upon impact Creep Spring is overcome, Striker fires Cap and explodes the Detonator, which in turn explodes the Grenade. Designed to explode on impact of any part of the exterior of this Grenade.
Hand only, 12-15 yards. Thrower must have adequate cover owing to terrific blast.	High penetration. Great Morale and Blast effect. Material effect is considerable on objects at point of burst.	Remove Lid. Insert Detonator closed end first. Replace Lid.	Remove Safety Cap of "All-ways" Fuse, Tape will unwind and pull out Pin during flight leaving Striker free to overcome Creep Spring. Explodes when any portion of Grenade strikes on firm material.

GRENADE

Type.	A. How Recognised when issued.	B. Description.	C. Type of Fuse and Ignition.	D. When, Where and How Grenade should be used.
6 No. 74. S.T. Hand Grenade. (Sticky).	Ball shaped, about five inches in diameter, Enclosed in Khaki painted Tin Outer Casing. Black Bakelite Handle. Practice : Wood Model, painted white, with steel band for correct weight.	Glass Flask. Filled with H.E. Protected by Metal Khaki Casing which is removed before using Grenade. Flask is covered by a sticky envelope. Inside neck of Flask is a Tube to hold a Detonator Assembly. A Black Bakelite Handle with a No. 36 type Striker is fitted. Weight 2¼ lbs. approximately.	5-second Fuse. Detonator and C.E. Pellet. 1¼ lbs. Nitro-Glycerine in Glass Flask.	Against all A.F.Vs. etc. Will adhere to target unless surface is steeply sloping, vertical, wet or muddy. Can be thrown from buildings on A.F.Vs. with good effect. Best if placed on target by hand or as a portable demolition set.
7 No. 75 & 75a. Known as the Hawkins Grenade or Grenade Mine	Buff in colour with 75 or 75a painted on Striker Plate. 75a has 80% explosive only. Practice : Dull Red with White Band at ends.	Is a Talcum Powder Tin fitted with a Metal Striker Plate or Platform on one side. Weight about 2¼ lbs.	Instantaneous. Explodes when crushed. (Minimum crushing weight about 2 cwts.). The Detonator Unit consists of an Igniter and Detonator. Two used with each Grenade. The Igniter is a Tin Plate Tube closed at one end by flattening, and is painted Red. A rubber band is rolled on the Igniter. The Detonator is an Aluminium Tube open at one end and smaller in diameter than Igniter. It must be handled carefully. 1¼ lbs. Ammonal and 4 ozs. Victor Powder.	To be placed in the pathway of an oncoming A.F.V. Can be used to form a mine field. Placed up to and within 2 ft. of each other, sympathetic explosion results. Best used in a "Necklace" to ensure contacting A.F.V. tracks or tyres when pulled across a road.
8 No. 76. S.I.P. (Self-Igniting Phosphorus).	Half Pint Clear Glass Bottle.	Red Cap, Hand. Green Cap, Hand or "Northover."	Instantaneous on breaking. (Percussion). Yellow Phosphorus, Benzene, Rubber, Latex and Water.	A.F.V.'s Lorries, etc., and all forms of Incendiarism. As temporary smoke screen.
9 No. 77. Smoke Grenade.				

SUMMARY CHART.

E. Range and Danger Area.	F. Type of Effects.	G. To Prepare and Prime.	H. Mechanism in Operation.
Approx. 20 yards hand thrown. Blast highly concentrated forward unless explodes in mid-air. Ensure adequate cover available within 5-seconds.	Penetration, Lethal Blast, Morale. If sticking to target will generally cut hole approximately its own diameter on reasonably heavy Steel.	Unscrew Bakelite Neck Ring to remove handle. Take out Plug and insert Detonator Assembly. Make sure Rubber Bands are in correct position on Detonator Set. Replace Handle ensuring Bakelite Ring is fully tightened, otherwise handle may break when thrown.	Hold Grenade head downwards. Remove Pin holding outer casing which falls off. Pull out Safety Pin marked "Danger." Lever flies off when thrown. Then same as 36 but Fuse 5-seconds. Make certain that the small circular Knurled Brass Nut in top of Handle is firmly in position before pulling Pin.
Hand only. About 20 yards. Container is light and disintegrates completely. Blast is Heavy. Danger area may be up to 75 yards.	Penetration, Blast Lethal, and Morale. Blast effect sideways and upwards.	Insert Igniter and Detonator, square cut end first. Do not remove Cap at end of Body.	The Grenade is shaped so that when thrown it will come to rest with the Striker Plate either on top or underneath. It will operate equally well in both positions. Is safe until run over and Striker Plate crushed. Do not touch to reclaim Grenade if dented or damaged. Remove ignition set when reclaimed.
Hand, about 20-30 yards. Northover, 75-150 yards. Immediately dangerous to wherever Liquid splashes.	Incendiary and Smoke.	Ready for use when issued.	If used for Incendiary purposes in Blitzed house, should have Detonator and Safety Fuse attached to side of the Bottle to ensure breaking.

CLASSIFICATION OF GRENADES.

Grenades can be classified into four classes.

(a) INSTRUCTIONAL GRENADES.

The use of these are for explanation of the mechanism of grenades, are very similar to drill grenades, very often sectioned, empty component parts being utilised, and the grenade is not weighted to bring it up to live weight.

To distinguish them they are painted similarly to live grenades, except that the red filling ring is not painted. They are packed in packages of service pattern over-stencilled with the following marks : (No. in each package), Grenades (Type), Instructional ( ), Mark ( ).

(b) GRENADES FOR DRILL PURPOSE.

These are prepared either for practice firing from a rifle or for throwing practice ; they are in every way similar to an actual live grenade, but sometimes have inert filling to obtain the correct weight.

For distinguishing purposes their colour is white, with the exception of No. 75 drill grenade, which is dull red. They are packed in boxes which have the following marks stencilled on them either in white or yellow : (No. in package), Grenade (Type), Drill No. ( ), Mark ( ).

(c) PRACTICE GRENADE.

The purpose of this grenade is that there should be an opportunity to use a grenade which can simulate the action of a live grenade. The variation from a live grenade is the charge, which is considerably reduced to avoid the possibility of serious accidents. This type has not been generally issued, therefore, special markings are not yet published.

(d) LIVE GRENADES.

Every type of live grenade which is filled with a charge for service use has a painted red band around it ; this may be either in the form of a series of red X's or alternatively a continuous band. The former type of marking denotes that the filling is suitable for storage in hot, humid climates without fear of deterioration taking place.

✠ " That's only a practice grenade ! " ✠

Occasionally live grenades have a band of another colour or other markings on them, in addition to the above, the purpose of this being for the information of the technical expert, to tell him the type of filling, etc.

No 36 MILLS GRENADE. (see sketches 1 and 1A).

Action : Anti-Personnel. **Fuse :** Time, 4 and 7 secs.

No. 36 Mills Grenades are issued packed 12 in a wooden box, marked with the words "*Hand Grenade*" and "*4 secs.*", A base plug key is usually clipped on the inside of the lid. In each box, separately packed, will be found a tin containing 12 Igniter Sets.

When grenades are intended for use with cup dischargers, the wooden case is marked "7 *secs.*" In the case are the necessary gas checks, also 14 ballastite cartridges as propellents for use in a specially strengthened rifle fitted with an E.Y. cup, and a tin containing 12 Igniter Sets separately packed.

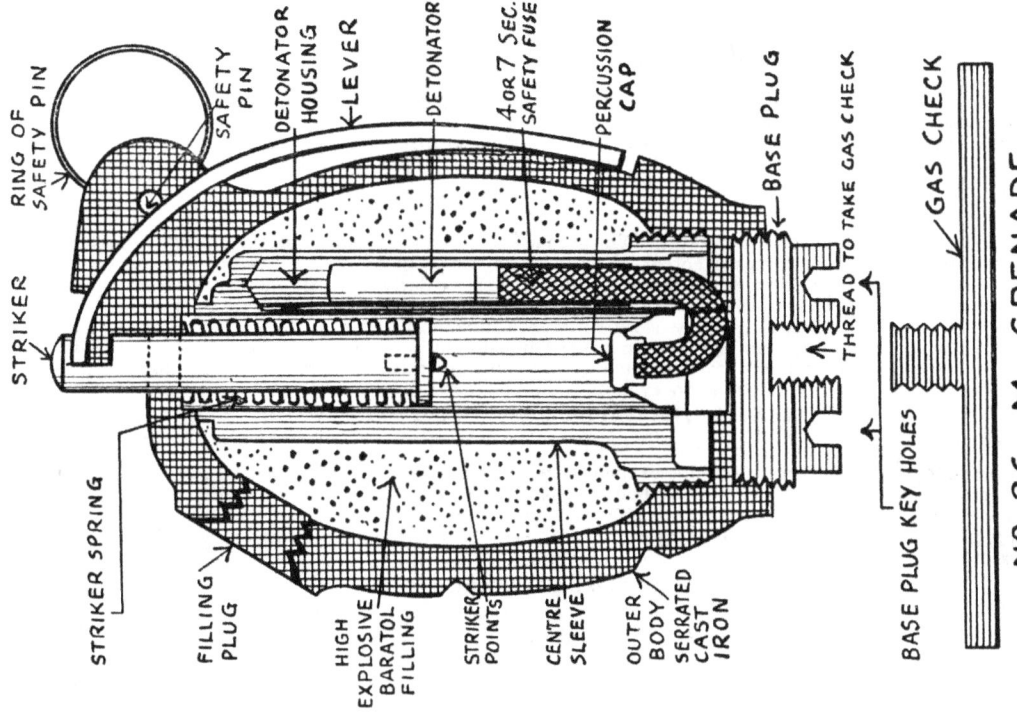

No. 36. M. GRENADE.
SKETCH 1.

This grenade can be used for a number of purposes, mainly anti-personnel, for killing the crews of A.F.V.'s, clearing enemy dug-outs and other forms of similar cover, clearing buildings, trenches, machine gun nests. etc. It proved itself in the 1914-1918 war, and is probably the best known and most successful of all grenades. The fuse timing and explosive content have been altered for the present war.

The grenade consists of an outer cast-iron body, serrated to assist fragmentation on explosion. Can be recognised from its similarity to a very small pineapple. In the middle of the body is a centre piece, which contains a spring and striker, with space for the igniter set. These two are maintained in place by a lever fitted in a slot at the striker top. The lever is held by a safety pin passing over it, through two holes in the two shoulders, which project from the outside of the body. The grenade is painted black, varnished, and has a red and/or green band of X's.

GENERAL

The No. 36 Mills Grenade is charged with baratol. The grenade is intended generally for the killing or wounding of personnel, being most dangerous in a radius of approximately 20-25 yards from the point of burst. Fragments have been known to cause casualties up to a distance of 100 yards from the point of bursting, particularly if a shrapnel burst is obtained.

The grenade weighs approximately 1¼ lbs. and can be thrown by hand about 30 yards. It is extremely useful in all types of close-quarter fighting, either in town or country areas. Before throwing, make absolutely certain you and members of your section or platoon are well under cover, or have taken cover immediately available after throwing. If the situation is such that no such cover is within reach, then the thrower must go flat, preferably feet towards explosion, hands protecting neck and back of skull, choosing if possible an indentation or hollow in the ground.

✠ " O.K. sir, Bill told me these are not primed ! " ✠

STRIPPING THE GRENADE.

Remove the base plug to ensure grenade is not primed, take out pin after closing the points, maintaining a firm hold on the lever to prevent it rising from its flush position in the body. Place the base plug end of the grenade against the body, and permit the lever to rise under control; shake out spring and striker. Remove all traces of wax (use paraffin in cold weather if available) from the striker, spring, body and central sleeve, making sure to see that the striker is quite straight and has two nipples with a vertical gap between them.

✠ " Nobody's looking, you can smoke ! " ✠

To check the striker for operation, fit with spring into the centre sleeve, with the slot at the striker top towards the shoulders. Force the striker through the grenade top, insert the lever in the slot, holding it down firmly with the base of the grenade against the body. Move the lever up and down several times, then release under control. This movement is to ensure the striker moving freely, also that the spring has enough tension to force the striker down to detonate the ·22 cap. Always reject a weak spring or one which tends to jam in the sleeve.

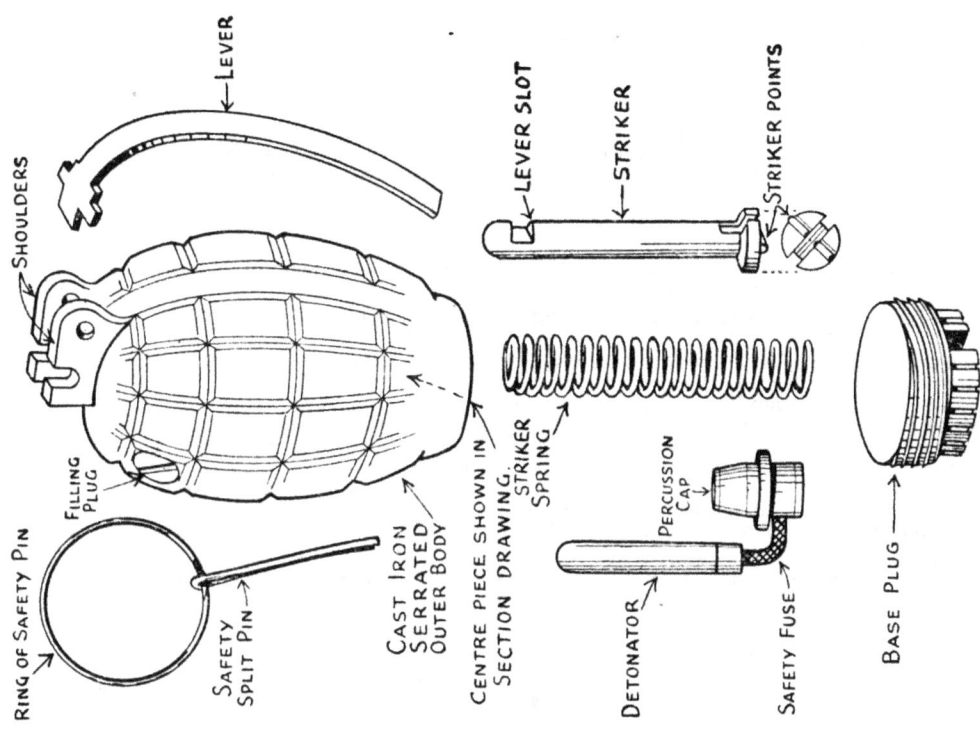

ASSEMBLY.
Refit the striker and spring in the sleeve as explained above; with the lever inserted and held securely with the fingers, hold the grenade with the filling screw nearest towards you, refit the pin. Should the grenade thrower be right-handed replace pin from right to left; if left-handed, the reverse way. Finally replace the base plug.

MECHANISM.
The actual sequence of operations which take place when using the grenade are as follows :—

When the pin is withdrawn and the grenade thrown, the spring presses down the striker, causing the lever to fly off. The ·22 cap is struck by the end of the striker, explodes, and ignites the fuse. This sets off the detonator, which detonates the charge in the grenade.

IGNITER SET.
The igniter set is the actual means of exploding the grenade; therefore, should be handled with the greatest care. Always take hold of it by the cap chamber or the fuse; avoid touching the detonator, which should never be TAPPED, HIT, STRUCK OR CRUSHED. Remember always to keep it away from any heat. DO NOT DISMANTLE THE IGNITER SET.

✠ " That's O.K. sir, I've handled detonators for years ! " ✠

The igniter set consists of a ·22 cap in a chamber with a short length of safety fuse, to which is fastened a detonator; the length of the fuse controls the time required for detonation.

When examining the igniter set, ensure the hole in the ·22 cap centre is covered and sealed, the cap chamber quite sound, with the cap chamber and detonator firmly fixed to the safety fuse itself.

There are two types of igniter sets. For hand throwing the fuse is 4 secs.; for recognition it is white in coloured, and has a rubber band which should never be removed. For the 36 grenade fired from an E.Y. Cup Discharger, a 7-sec. fuse is generally used; this fuse is yellow, without a rubber band. The same usually applies if fired from a Northover Projector, but under certain circumstances the 4-sec. fuse can be used (shrapnel effect, etc.). Always use a Cup Discharger in preference to a Northover if available, but if firing from a Northover remember to REMOVE rubber shock pad from the propellent.

TO PRIME THE GRENADE.
Undo the base plug with the tool provided (base plug key), check the detonator sleeve to make certain it is free from any rough edges. Fit the cap chamber and detonator by inserting as far as possible into their respective sleeves without using any undue force. Finally refit and tighten base plug.

✠ " Don't fumble, shove it in." ✠

It may occasionally be necessary to bend the fuse, so as to assist easy insertion. This can best be done by taking hold of the fuse and cap chamber between two fingers and pressing gently together.

GRENADE THROWING

Position 1. Ready
SKETCH 2.

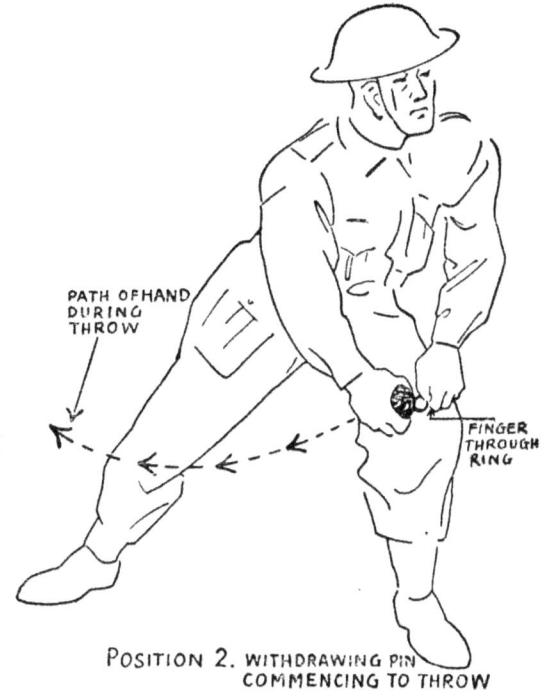

Position 2. Withdrawing pin commencing to throw
SKETCH 3.

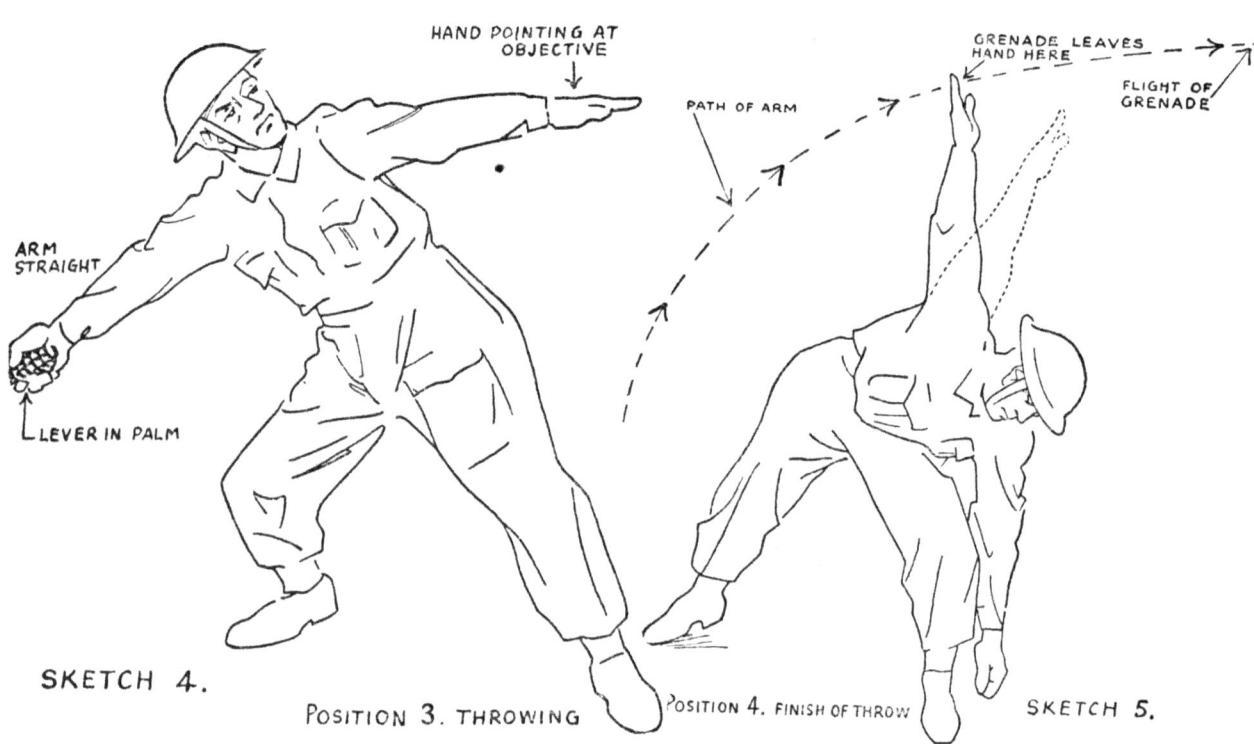

Certain safety precautions must be taken when handling these grenades for examination or demonstration purposes. First, always remove the base plug to assure the grenade is not primed. Before throwing, make certain the grenade is in working order by noting if the lever is quite secure in the striker slot, also if it lies flush with the grenade body. Should this not be the case, the lever can usually be fitted flush when the grenade is being stripped.

✠ " Don't bother to check, we haven't got time ! " ✠

Always make sure that neither of the shoulders are cracked, broken or chipped, and the safety pin sound and not too loose.

SKETCH 6.

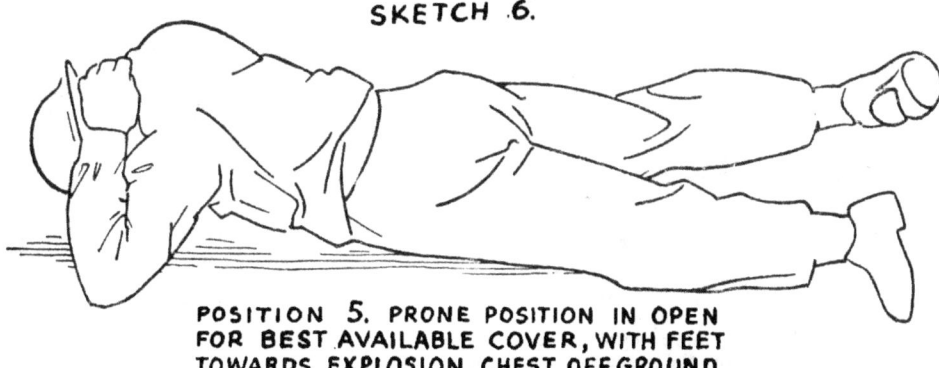

POSITION 5. PRONE POSITION IN OPEN FOR BEST AVAILABLE COVER, WITH FEET TOWARDS EXPLOSION, CHEST OFF GROUND.

CORRECT METHODS OF THROWING GRENADE. (See sketches 2, 3, 4, 5 and 6).

This grenade is very difficult to throw by the average man in the normal meaning. To obtain the best effects, the grenade should be delivered at a high angle by utilising a good overarm swing, which can be likened to that of bowling in cricket, except more elevation is required. In town fighting this type of throwing is often impossible, so unorthodox throwing should be practiced. Accuracy must be the first consideration ; this can only be obtained by the use of a quite natural, vigorous swinging motion of the arm, with plenty of practice. The correct manner to hold the grenade for actual use is as follows : Hold it in the right hand with base pointing downwards, the lever being placed along the inside of the fingers, the thumb being

✠ " I prefer to hold the lever under my thumb ! " ✠

just beneath the filling screw ; hold the grenade firmly. Face the target, turn to the right, move the left foot so that it points towards the target, at the same time balance the body. Glance behind to ensure the right arm and hand have freedom of movement. Keep the left arm quite straight near to the body, hand at left knee, finger through the safty pin ring, knuckles outwards ; take out the pin by moving the right hand downwards and backwards with a vigorous motion, at the same time fixing your eyes on the target ; swing back as far as possible, permitting the left arm to come up naturally. Without pausing, swing rapidly forward, maintaining the right arm rigid, throw the grenade, pause to observe accuracy of throw, etc. (not more than 3 secs.), then take cover. If the thrower is left-handed all the motions above will be reversed.

✠ " I never slip, sir ! " ✠

To enable the thrower to obtain practice in throwing the grenade from many different types of cover, training should be given in throwing from a bank, behind a wall, a trench, etc. Naturally, the position of the thrower must be altered or modified to suit the particular type of cover available and its height, possibly requiring a leaning or lying position. Always check and observe the direction of the target first, particularly before attempting to throw from " blind " cover. In many cases it may be necessary to " drop " or " lob " the grenade, probably under hand, when attacking A.F.V's, windows, or an opening in a wall, etc. Practice high-angle throwing. Practice with the left hand, as obviously many occasions will arise when right-hand throwing would be impossible without exposing the body ; this particularly applies in town fighting.

USE OF CUP DISCHARGER.

When practising for house clearing get used to counting the seconds up to when the grenade should explode. Quite often even four seconds can be too long, sometimes making it necessary to hold the grenade for perhaps two seconds **after** the lever is released, to ensure it exploding instantly, in say, an adjoining room, when pushed through a hole in the wall. Shortage of four second fuses may compel the use of seven second fuses. The enemy are fully aware of the timing of most of our grenades, therefore a man seeing a grenade arrive in the room from which he cannot readily escape or find cover, would realise he is almost certain to be killed if he allows the grenade to explode in the room. He would most likely take the chance of there being one or more seconds to spare and either throw the grenade back or out of a window.

Automatically counting the seconds enables you to " observe " without fluster, and time your next move or rush to a fraction, whilst the enemy if not killed, would still be suffering from shock, or unable to see you because of dust, smoke, etc.

Almost accurate counting can be attained as follows :—Repeat steadily, " one second, two second, three second," and so on ; or " one and two and three and " etc.

Among the many tricks in town fighting, too numerous to mention here, the ability to get a grenade into a room either one or more floors below should be practised. The majority of houses have about ten feet between floors, so about fifteen feet or more of card or string is required. Tie any weight to the end, lower to one side of your objective so the weight shall not be seen to enable the length of string required to be ascertained, or measure roughly the height of the room from which the grenade is to be thrown and add to this length the distance from window centre to ceiling. Fit a gas check to the grenade to which the string can be tied. Hold the string at the point of the length you have measured, in the left hand, withdraw the pin and throw the grenade straight outwards. When the grenade has reached the end of the travel allowed by the length of string, it will swing downwards. As soon as you feel the string strike the top edge of the window below, the grenade should have entered the room, then release the string **immediately** to ensure the burst taking place well back into the room. If thrown from one floor only this will keep the grenade in the air long enough for the fuse to function fully. If you do not release the string the grenade will probably swing out again and burst in the open. This method can be used with other grenades but remember blast and splinters also travel upwards, take precautions accordingly if your floor is very thin.

The discharger is used to obtain greater range with reasonable accuracy, when such range is required for the 36 M.; also to discharge the 68 A.T. Grenade. It is known as the E.Y. Cup Discharger, and is fitted to a specially strengthened rifle. The propellant used in the rifle is a ballistic cartridge. There are a number of safety precautions that are always to be observed when firing a grenade from a rifle fitted with a discharger. These are as follows: Be absolutely certain that ballastite cartridges only are used. They can be distinguished in the case of the ·303 calibre by the fact that half of the length of the cartridge is blackened and no bullet fitted. The rimless ·300 ballistite has no distinguishing mark, but the end of the cartridge is crimped,

✠ "It doesn't matter! I heard Ballistite is only a trade name for Ball Ammunition." ✠

and of course no bullet fitted. Secondly, NEVER USE BALL AMMUNITION to discharge a grenade from a rifle fitted with a discharger, as a serious accident will occur. It is only in the greatest emergency that ball ammunition should be fired through the empty discharger, then only at close range.

DESCRIPTION OF DISCHARGER No. 1. (see sketches 7 and 7A),

This discharger is intended for fitting to, and for use with, the No. 1 Rifle, i.e., the Short Magazine Lee Enfield (S.M.L.E.). The barrel of the discharger is cylindrical and has a screw thread fitted internally to enable it to receive the locking base. Close to the lower end is a slot which actually forms the gas port; this slot in turn may be closed by a sliding shutter which, after adjustment to the required opening, can be fixed in position by a clamping nut. The locking base is screw threaded on its outside, to fit the barrel. It has a central hole which is threaded, to enable it to receive the adjusting screw, the point has a slot so that it can be tightened by the point of a bayonet. Tighten in a clockwise direction. Below these are two claw-type levers; these are intended for engagement of the slotted sides of the rifle nose cap.

When it is intended to fire a No. 36 Grenade from a Cup Discharger, the igniter set used generally has a 7-sec. fuse fitted to it. It may be necessary in street fighting to fire a grenade into a small window, or for some similar purpose, in which case it might be advisable to use a 4-sec. fuse. Practice this, timing the flight of the grenade at short ranges at difficult objectives. A high degree of accuracy can soon be attained.

Boxes containing this type of igniter set are plainly marked, being stencilled "7 secs." on the outside; the fuse itself **differs** from the 4-sec. fuse by being coloured yellow, without a rubber band.

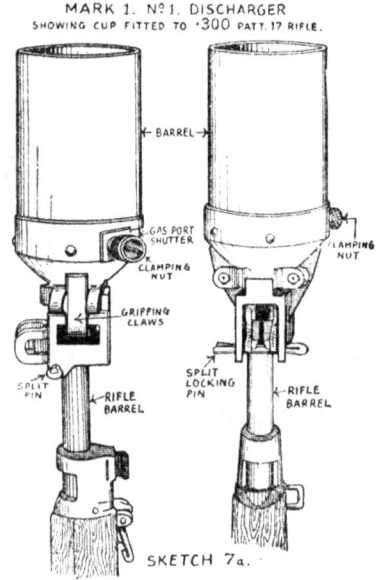

SKETCH 7a.

MARK 1. Nº 1. DISCHARGER
SHOWING CUP FITTED TO ·300 PATT. 17 RIFLE.

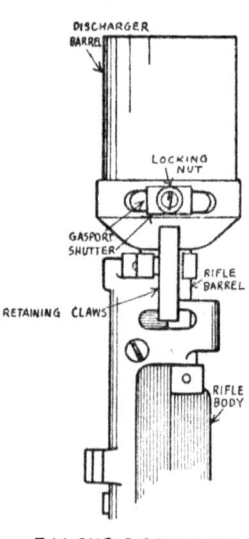

E.Y. CUP DISCHARGER
M.K.I. FITTED TO S.M.L.E.
SKETCH 7.

HOW TO ATTACH THE DISCHARGER.

To attach the discharger, unscrew the locking base for approximately three turns, making certain that the adjusting screw is also screwed back about ⅛ inch within the locking base face. Fit the discharger on the rifle nose cap, with the large recess in the locking base facing the bayonet boss. Then screw the barrel tightly down on to the locking base, fit the bayonet point into the mouth of the barrel, to engage it in the adjusting screw slots, then screw it in a right-hand direction until it is sufficiently tight. During the fixing of the cup whilst standing or sitting, it is advisable to hold the rifle barrel outwards between the knees.

HOW TO DETACH THE DISCHARGER.

Unscrew two or three turns, then by sliding the thumb and forefinger of the left hand on to the claw lever's upper ends it is possible to press it inwards and lift the discharger off the rifle nose cap.

CLEANING THE DISCHARGER.

To clean the discharger, commence by unscrewing the locking base and adjusting screw ; then wipe the inside of the barrel and all surfaces of the shutter with a clean dry rag, so as to remove any traces of fouling. Continue cleaning by utilising an oiled rag ; finally, dry again and oil.

The adjusting screw and locking base are cleaned in a similar manner, at the same time paying special attention to the actual threads themselves, as these are liable to become dirty, making it extremely difficult to attach or detach the discharger in an emergency. Finally, reassemble. Should the discharger be affected in any way by gas, clean it by the same methods taught you for cleaning the rifle under the same conditions.

HOW TO LOAD THE No. 36 GRENADE.

When firing a No. 36 Grenade from a discharger, it is always necessary to have a gas check fitted, screwed tightly in position in the base plug. The grenade should then be inserted in the discharger, gas check FIRST. Care must be taken to ensure that the striker lever itself is inside the discharger before the pin is withdrawn ; should the lever be left on the outside a serious acccide would be certain 7 or 4 secs. after the pin was withdrawn unless the rifle were fired immediately. The pin can then be withdrawn and the grenade finally pushed down as far as it will go.

In the event of the opportunity of firing having passed, it is quite in order to replace the pin, but this must be done definitely before removing the grenade from the discharger after applying the safety catch of the rifle. Do not unload the rifle first, as the grenade might accidentally fall out of the cup.

HOW TO USE THE DISCHARGER FOR No. 36 GRENADE.

When discharging a No. 36 Grenade from an E.Y. fitted rifle, the rifle is held at an angle of 45°, leaning towards the target, with the butt heel on the ground if soft, or on a sandbag for hard surfaces. (**See Sketch No. 8**). The grenade can also be discharged by firing from the hip. See precautions and methods on later page.

Set out below are the approximate ranges which may be obtained when the rifle is leaning at the above angle, and the variations in them that are possible by closing or opening the gas port :—

　75– 85 yards approximately. Gas port fully open.
　105–115　　,,　　　　,,　　　　,,　　one-quarter closed.
　130–150　　,,　　　　,,　　　　,,　　one-half closed.
　165–180　　,,　　　　,,　　　　,,　　three-quarters closed.
　195–210　　,,　　　　,,　　　　,,　　fully closed.

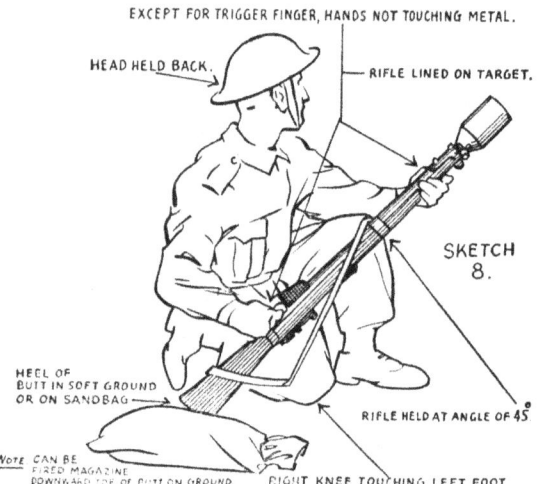

SKETCH 8.

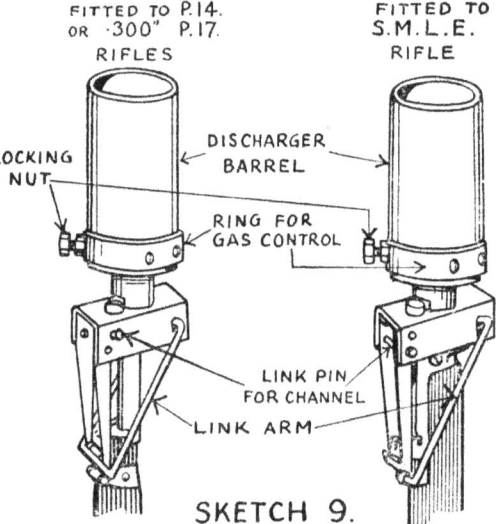

SKETCH 9.

Nº 2 MARK 1 CUP DISCHARGER

The above approximate ranges do not allow for tail or head winds; these should, therefore, be allowed for when they prevail. With regard to the actual gas port openings above, all measurements for such openings must be taken from the inside edge of the shutter; in other words, the actual effective area. Owing to the high trajectory of the grenade when fired from a rifle at 45°, the flight is considerably affected by cross winds; allowance must be made accordingly.

No. II DISCHARGER, MARK I.

This pattern of discharger is intended for use with either the .300 Pat. 17 Rifle, No. 3 Rifle pattern 14, or the No. 1 .303 S.M.L.E.

DETAILS OF THE No. II DISCHARGER, MARK I. (See sketch 9).

The discharger barrel is fitted with a ring for regulating the gas so as to obtain difference of range.

It should be noted that when the No. 68 Grenade is used with either types of dischargers, **all gas ports must be fully closed**. The barrel itself screws into the base on one end of which will be seen two sets of holes, one marked No. 1 and the other P.14.

The channel link should be fitted to the base by means of the channel link pin if the discharger is used with the No. 1 Rifle. It is important that the channel link should be fitted to the base by inserting the pin through the No. 1 hole, then through the bottom of the two holes in the channel link. On the other hand, should the discharger be required for use with the Pat. 17 or Pat. 14 Rifle, the P.14 hole in this case must be used, at the same time using only the top hole in the channel link. To fix the discharger, unscrew it about six turns from the base, then carefully place into position the channel link placed over the bayonet standard. Drop the link beneath the channel link, finally screw down the discharger approximately finger tight. Never use excessive force, as serious damage might be caused to the rifle barrel.

To detach the discharger unscrew, lift the link and channel link, then remove it completely.

The same care, attention and instructions as those given for the No. 1 Discharger should be used when cleaning **the** No. II Discharger.

HOW TO FIRE A No. 36 GRENADE FROM A No. II DISCHARGER.

The procedure is the same as when firing from a No. I Mark I as described previously, but the range is altered by varying the gas regulator ring. This ring has four holes which by rotation may be made to coincide with your similar holes in the barrel, or alternatively with any less number that may be required. The approximate ranges obtained by exposing one or more holes in the barrel, or having them all closed, are given as follows. (No allowance is made for wind variations.)

With the four holes uncovered range is approx. 75–85 yards.
,, three ,, ,, ,, ,, 105–115 ,,
,, two ,, ,, ,, ,, 130–150 ,,
,, one ,, ,, ,, ,, 165–180 ,,
,, all ,, covered ,, ,, 195–210 ,,

To obtain these ranges, all that is necessary is to undo the locking bolt, turn the ring until the required number of holes are covered or uncovered, then retighten the bolt.

No. 68 GRENADE. (See sketch 10).

Action : Penetration.   **Fuse :** Percussion.   Instantaneous explosion on impact.

No. 68 Grenades, when issued for service use, are supplied packed in a metal box, which contains 17 grenades and 20 rounds of ballastite cartridges as propellants. All live grenades of this class are issued ready for service use; they MUST NOT be stripped, except by technical experts.

This is a penetration grenade, invented and introduced to the service with the particular object of blowing holes into or otherwise damaging A.F.V's, and in some instances for demolition.

It is intended for firing from a discharger with a ballastite cartridge as propellent; its effective range is approximately 50–75 yards. When firing the No. 68 Grenade always make certain that the gas port or ports are completely closed. The sights fitted to the rifle are specially designed for use between these particular distances.

Always endeavour to hit the most vulnerable portion of A.F.V's, which in tanks is generally in the rear, as armour there is usually thinner.

Under certain conditions this type of grenade can be fired from the hip with a rifle fitted with a discharger. This is particularly useful in certain types of town fighting, remembering always that this grenade is not anti-personnel. The grenade weighs approximately 1¾ lbs.

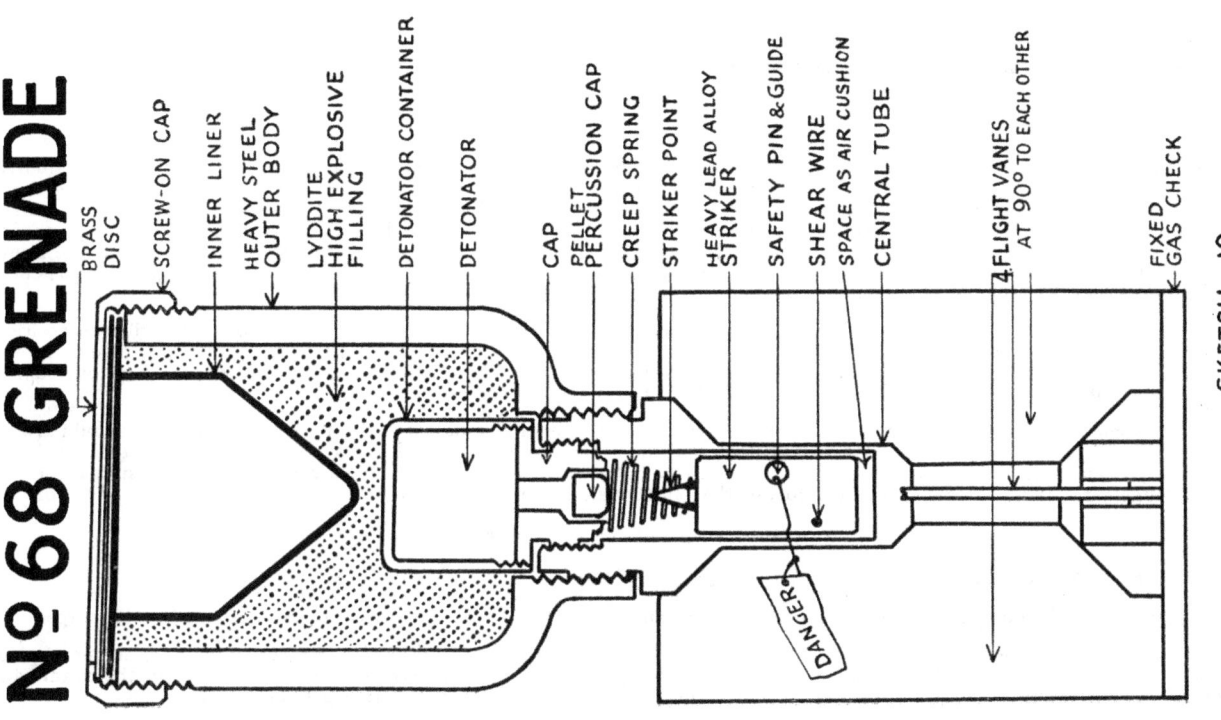

DESCRIPTION OF GRENADE.

The top of the grenade is filled with H.E., or 6½ ozs. of Lyddite, contained in a thick metal alloy casing sealed at its front by means of a brass disc held in place by a screwed ring. It is painted buff with red and green bands around the body.

DETAILS AND MECHANICAL ACTION.

The tail portion or unit has vanes fitted to it, to enable the grenade to maintain accuracy in flight to ensure the explosive container striking the target first. This is necessary as the striker in this type of instantaneous fuse will only function if it can move suddenly forward towards the head of the grenade. The tail also contains a hollow central sleeve in which is fitted a creep spring and the striker. The striker itself is maintained in place by a safety pin, which has a label attached to it, marked " To be withdrawn from grenade before firing " ; secondly, by means of a shear wire, both fitted to and through the sleeve A gas check is usually bolted to the end of the tail fins. The grenade **must** always be placed in the discharger with gas check FIRST, otherwise the grenade will burst instantaneously when the ballastite cartridge is fired.

Prior to firing, the safety pin is taken out, leaving the shear wire and creep spring only to hold the striker in position. On being fired from a rifle the shock of discharge jerks the heavy striker backwards, thus cutting the shear wire. Detonation is caused by the sudden stopping of forward flight through striking a solid object, forcing the striker to jerk forward, overcoming the resistance of the creep spring and firing the detonator which explodes the grenade.

It has sometimes been recommended that this grenade be used from a Northover Projector, but the E.Y. cup should always be used in preference if available. More often than not there is insufficient initial shock of discharge from the Northover propellent to cause the shear wire holding the striker to be cut, with the result that unless a direct hit is registered, the fuse will not function. If it is found necessary to use the Northover, **do not forget** to remove the rubber shock pad from the propellent.

MARK I No. 68 GRENADE SIGHT. (See sketch 9a & 9b).

This is attached to enable accuracy to be obtained when firing a No. 68 Grenade from a rifle fitted with a discharger.

To fit the sight to the rifle, turn the back sight leaf over completely towards the rifle muzzle, undo the wing nuts and place the bar at the sight base in between the ramps of the back sight with the sight fixed leaf facing to the front, the metal band itself passing round the woodwork. Tighten up both wing nuts evenly to obtain the same pressure on the band.

MARK 1 N° "68" GRENADE SIGHT FOR USE WITH N°1 RIFLE FITTED WITH E.Y. CUP DISCHARGER.

SKETCH 9ª

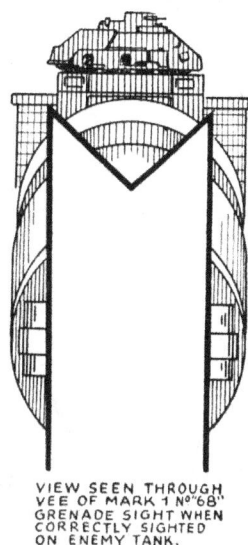

VIEW SEEN THROUGH VEE OF MARK 1 N° 68 GRENADE SIGHT WHEN CORRECTLY SIGHTED ON ENEMY TANK.

SKETCH 9ᵇ

For the P.17 and No. 3 Rifle a Mark II sight is utilised. To fit this, place it in front of the outer band. This type of sight can also be used on the No. 1 Rifle, but to use it for this rifle it should be fitted immediately to the rear of the outer band.

The topmost step is intended for use when aiming with a No. 3 Rifle, and the bottom one when aiming with the P.17 Rifle.

TO LOAD AND FIRE. (See sketch 11).

   Take out the safety pin. Do not throw it away, as a moving target often will be out of sight or range before the opportunity to fire occurs. Should this happen, replace the pin and the grenade is ready for further use.

SKETCH 11. HOW TO HOLD AND SUPPORT RIFLE AGAINST SANDBAG WHEN USING E.Y CUP DISCHARGER, FROM PRONE POSITION FIRING Nº '68' GRENADE

   Having removed the pin, fit the grenade into the discharger with THE GAS CHECK IN FIRST; push it fully home without any undue force. When actually firing, place yourself in such a position as to enable the rifle to be held at a flat angle. (See Sketch No. 11.) Probably the best position is for the firer to lie in the prone position with the left hand holding the rifle in front of the outer band. Always use some form of shock absorber for the butt of the rifle, as very considerable recoil shock takes place, due to using the high-powered ballastite cartridge, the resistance of the gas check and grenade against the escape of the expanding gases. It is suggested that a sandbag three-quarters filled should be used to take up the this shock; if not available, lumps of earth or a small hole in the ground to take the toe of the butt will serve the same purpose. For certain forms of attack or practice the 68 can be fired from the hip, but make sure **no** portion of the rifle touches the body. When

✠ " Rot, old boy, grenades don't mean a thing to me ! " ✠

firing, first push forward the safety catch, clench the right hand, at the same time placing the forefinger on the trigger. This finger should be the **only** portion of the body touching any metal part of the rifle. DO NOT TOUCH OR HOLD ANY METAL PART OF THE RIFLE EXCEPT THIS FINGER, IRRESPECTIVE OF THE POSITION DECIDED UPON FOR FIRING. This precaution is primarily to avoid burning. To aim correctly the head of the firer should be kept well back so he may be able to use the sights to the best advantage. Always aim and fire rapidly, as a moving target will soon be out of range; observe carefully the result of the shot, particularly if further correction for wind is required. Should the grenade not be fired, remove it from the discharger, replace the safety pin; it is then ready for further use. To get the maximum proficiency, practice and/or demonstrations should be carried out from various types of cover, such as slit trenches, windows of houses, pill boxes, etc. It has been found in practice when correct impact is obtained, i.e., heat first, the resultant extremely heavy forward blast will generally perforate the armour of light, medium and sometimes heavy tanks. This heavy forward explosion is due to the design of the explosive container of the grenade, as explained previously, and the type of explosive used.

USING THE GRENADE. (See sketch 12).

When aiming the grenade it is essential that the special sight should be used. The top of the grenade should approximately just close the " V " gap of the sight, aiming at the centre of the target. If the vehicle in question happens to be travelling across the front of the firer, the aim should be taken at a point ahead, the distance ahead being decided by the speed of the A.F.V. and how far the firer is from it. Allowance must, of course, be made for cross winds, but as the trejectory or flight of the 68 must be flat, the allowance is very small compared to the cross-wind correction required for the 36, which is usually fired at an angle of 45°.

Try and avoid the " 68 " striking any sloping or rounded surface, to prevent not only the grenade from roccocheting, but also to stop the forward blast of the explosion from being deflected, and so wasted. Aim should be taken to ensure the flat head of the grenade striking its objective as squarely as possible, enabling the blast to strike in a small forward restricted area without escaping through the grenade striking at an angle.

When a riccochet is caused, the grenade is deflected from its course, and in turning in its new direction of travel it invariably catches the tail on the target making it break away from the main body. As the striker is contained in the tail, the portion containing the explosive becomes useless. These facts should be carefully explained to recruits or students who, quite often are disappointed in the performance of the " 68," without realising the reason for failures.

✠ **" Don't bother about the red flags ! "** ✠

A cross wind will often cause riccochets, the relatively slow speed at which the grenade travels traps the wind in the vanes of the tail and fixed gas check, resulting in the grenade developing a " wobble." It will then probably strike its target on the edge of the explosive container; although detonation may take place the blast will be deflected and so lose most of its cutting effect. Try to aim directly into the wind at the target, although a little distance may be lost through wind resistance, the grenade will maintain a much steadier flight.

Continually using maximum range is another reason for some failures, because by the time the grenade reaches its objective, the nose has started to fall, generally causing a ricochet into the ground either of the grenade or the blast. A hit whilst in level flight invariably gives good results.

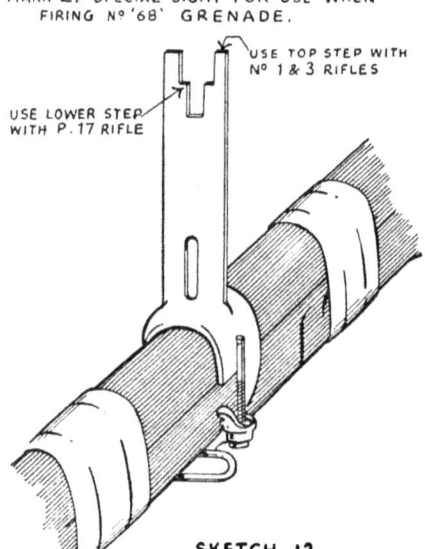

MARK 2. SPECIAL SIGHT FOR USE WHEN FIRING Nº '68' GRENADE.

USE TOP STEP WITH Nº 1 & 3 RIFLES

USE LOWER STEP WITH P.17 RIFLE

SKETCH 12.

WARNING.

Although this is not an anti-personnel grenade, it must be realised that the maximum range at which it can be used is only about 75 yards, therefore there is considerable danger from flying fragments of the tail unit. Pieces of this have been picked up as far as 100 yards from point of burst. It does not necessarily mean these fragments would be lethal, but instructors should take precautions accordingly. The fragments usually fly with a high trajectory, so that all those taking part in the practice should be fairly safe in the prone position.

THE No. 69 GRENADE. (See sketch 13).
Action : Blast. Morale. **Fuse** : Percussion, " All Ways."

These grenades are packed for service use in boxes holding 34, which in turn contain two small boxes holding 17 detonators each. The bakelite outer casing is black, with coloured markings on it, which may either be a band coloured red or red crosses around the top of the body. The body of the grenade has a milled band to help in maintaining a firm grip, but otherwise the surface is smooth and its shape is somewhat similar to the No. 36 M.

The No. 69 Bakelite Grenade has been designed as a light percussion hand grenade, relying almost entirely on blast for its offensive action. It has certain advantages. The lethal area of burst is very restricted ; therefore, it can easily be thrown while standing in the open without any real necessity for taking cover of any type, but always cover the eyes before the grenade bursts, as injury may occur due to flying fragments of bakelite. On account of its light weight, about ¾ lb., it can be thrown much further than the No. 36 M. Grenade. Although the material lethal damage is extremely small, its moral effect can be very considerable, especially when it is used at night, as in the darkness the vivid flash of the explosion causes momentary blindness, which, together with temporary deafness from the sharp report, tends to create a feeling of panic. Being unable to see or hear, the particular man concerned could quite easily believe himself to be the only survivor from a high explosive grenade. The best uses for this grenade are all forms of night patrols or actions, wherever such action is required to cause confusion. In town fighting, if thrown during dry or dusty weather it will raise a cloud of dust to cover movement if no smoke generators are available. It has proved itself extremely useful when necessary to clear rooms, etc., as in confined spaces, such as these, the explosion can have quite considerable effect.

The " 69 " can also be used as an " aid to realism " during manœuvres, introducing the effect of being under fire from live H.E. grenades without very much danger of injuries taking place. It is recommended when used for such exercises they should be thrown to the rear of the troops instead of in front of them, if possible into ditches or holes besides the roads, to assist in

✠ **" Chuck it over, I won't miss it ! "** ✠

preventing accidents. Do not use this type of grenade either whilst on night manœuvres, as men might not be seen, or close to advancing troops. Fragments of the bakelite and the lead ball, which is contained in the fuse, can under these circumstances cause accidents. As a safety factor this type of grenade should be regarded as having a danger area of at least 35 yards when used on exercises.

✠ **" I can easily throw it through that window without being seen ! "** ✠

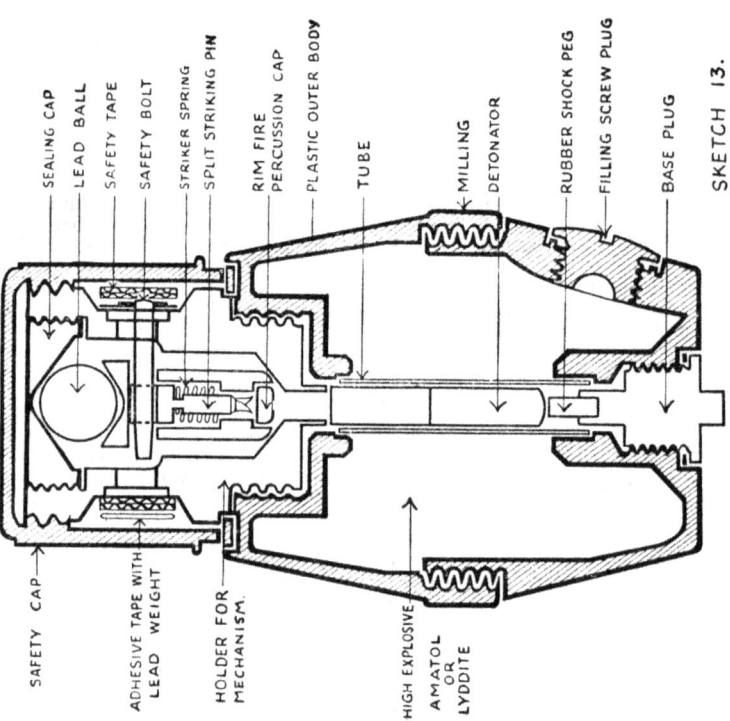

SKETCH 13.

MECHANICAL DETAILS OF THE " 69 " GRENADE. (See sketch 14).

After removing the safety cap it is essential, as a safety precaution, to hold the safety tape in position by the thumb and forefinger until the grenade is thrown ; when thrown the weight causes the tape to unwind and pull out the safety bolt. The striker is then only prevented from hitting the firing cap by the creep spring. When the grenade hits the object or the ground

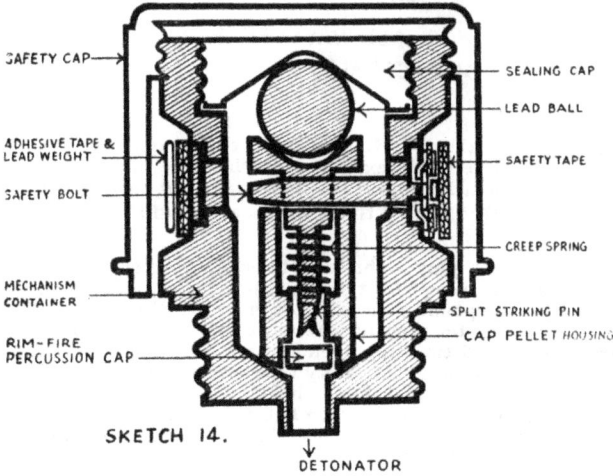

near the object which it is intended to attack, the impact causes the lead ball to push the striker down with sufficient force to overcome the tension of the creep spring, explodes the cap which fires the detonator, and in turn explodes the grenade. This type of fuse is generally known as an " ALL WAYS FUSE " because, no matter how the grenade lands, it should always explode. NOTE.—Although the tape may unwind even to the extent of withdrawing the safety bolt, the grenade will not burst until it receives some slight jar or shock. It can be placed in any position, but DO NOT ATTEMPT to throw once the safety bolt is withdrawn. (See sketch 15).

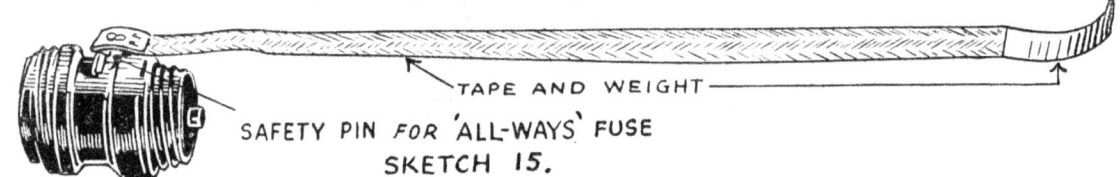

SAFETY PIN FOR 'ALL-WAYS' FUSE
SKETCH 15.

WARNING.

If used for practice or as an " aid to realism " ALL " blinds " or unexploded grenades MUST be found and destroyed, as if kicked or stepped on they will almost certainly explode with this type of fuse. The result of such an explosion at close range would undoubtedly be fatal. Naturally, this applies to **all** grenades, but particularly to those fitted with " All-ways " fuses.

✠" I don't think that's a ' blind ! ' "✠

SAFETY DETAILS.

When handling, always remove the base plug ; check to be sure the grenade is not primed. Live grenades issued for service use are in every way ready for action, except for the actual priming ; they must never be stripped. The grenade has an outer body manufactured from a plastic compound generally known as bakelite ; this is filled with high explosive which may be either amatol or lyddite. The safety cap of the grenade is retained securely in position by a piece of adhesive tape ; to remove the safety cap all that is necessary is to pull off this tape, then unscrew the cap approximately half a turn. It is not advised to unscrew more than this, as it is quite easy to unwind the safety tape which is underneath. Inside the cap is a mechanism holder which contains a striker, a lead ball, a creep spring, and the cap holder with cap. A safety peg or bolt passes through an aperture in the striker, also through a similar aperture in the mechanism holder, which prevents the striker from moving. The safety bolt has one end of a length of tape fitted to it, on the other end of which is attached a light lead weight, whilst, through the centre of the grenade is fitted a sleeve to hold the detonator.

INSTRUCTIONS FOR PRIMING.

Take off the base plug and check the detonator sleeve to make certain it is free from any obstructions, rough edges or burrs. Fit the detonator in with the open end first. Replace the base plug, making certain it is screwed home as far as possible.

INSTRUCTION FOR THROWING.

Due to its light weight it can be thrown as in ordinary throwing, but one of the best methods is to use the same overarm throw as for the No. 36 M.; alternatively, it may be lobbed or thrown underarm. If it is being lobbed over a short distance, it is advisable that a twist or turn should be given to this type of grenade so as to make certain the tape unwinds fully and falls clear, withdrawing the safety bolt with it. Can be thrown approximately 40 yards.

THE No. 73 ANTI-TANK GRENADE. (See sketch 16).

Action : Heavy blast. **Fuse :** Percussion, "All Ways."

Otherwise known as the "Thermos Flask" grenade.

These grenades when supplied for service use are packed in tin boxes containing 10. In the same box is a cylindrical container holding 10 detonators.

The "73" was primarily designed with the object of causing damage to A.F.V's, the best results being obtained when it is used against the suspension or tracks of a tank. This grenade is very useful in town fighting owing to its high explosive content. Dropped from roofs or windows, either singly or in numbers tied together, it can have disastrous results to A.F.V's or other vehicles. With a little ingenuity, again single or in numbers, a very effective mine can be made. In town fighting its wide blast range can readily be avoided as there are always walls, window sills, areas and other forms of adequate cover almost always available. It weighs approximately 4 lbs. Due to its weight, its shape and form, it will be found in practice it can only be thrown for quite short distances, i.e., approximately 10 to 16 yards.

✠ " Let's walk over, nobody is throwing from the ' bays ' ! " ✠

It contains a considerable amount of very powerful explosive. It, therefore, **must** be impressed upon the thrower to take adequate cover.

SAFETY.

Always check to see the grenade is not primed

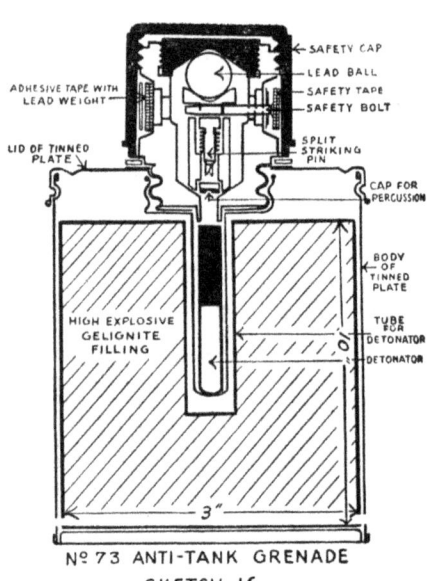

No. 73 ANTI-TANK GRENADE
SKETCH 16.

No 74 GRENADE (S.T.)
"STICKY BOMB."

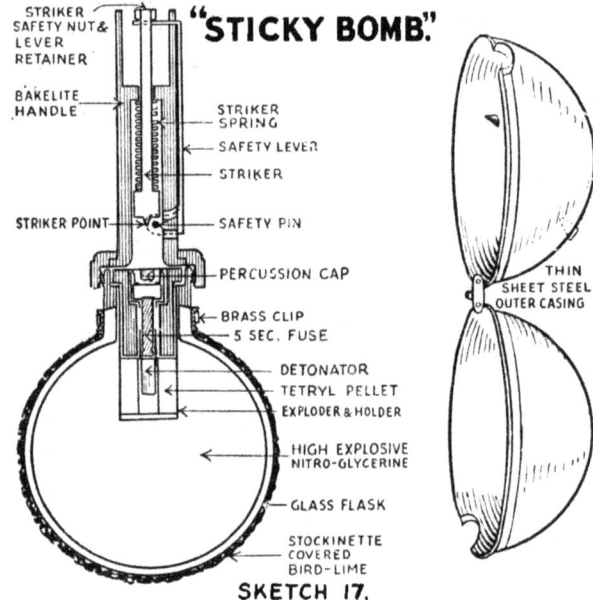

SKETCH 17.

DETAILS.

The No. 73 Grenade consists of a thin tinned outer casing which has a screw-on pattern cap of similar material at the top. To the centre of the lid is attached a mechanism holder, which in turn contains an "All Ways" contact fuse identical to that fitted to the No. 69 Grenade. The main body of the grenade is filled with 3¼ lbs. of gelignite or dynamite. It will, therefore, be realised that when detonated a violent explosion of great destructive power results. The body is coloured buff, whilst the top cap is black. The body has a red band round it and is stencilled with the mark "73 A.T." The grenade is approximately 10 inches in height by 3 inches in diameter.

PRIMING.

Take off the adhesive tape from the lip of the top lid, unscrew the lid, at the same time keeping the safety cap in position. On the underside of the lid will be found a tube; this should be unscrewed from the lid and checked to see if it is entirely free from obstruction, burrs or other damage. After examining the tube, fit the detonator into it with the closed end first; or, in other words, the **open** end of the detonator should appear at the **open** end of the tube. Finally, screw the tube containing the detonator back into position on the underside of the lid; then rescrew the lid itself back in position, finger tight. Take great care to enter the detonator tube centrally in the hole which is made to receive it in the explosive. The grenade is now live and ready for use. It may be found that the top lid tends to jam or slip, due to the threads on the body being either crossed or torn. If this should be the case, a piece of string or material, or any small strips of soft paper, should be laid on the threads on the body; it will then be possible for the top lid to be screwed down and maintain a good grip.

MECHANISM OF FUSE.

Exactly as in the No. "69." (**See sketch No. 14**).

METHOD OF USING AND THROWING THE GRENADE.

Remove the adhesive tape which holds the safety cap in place; then take off the safety cap itself. After removing the safety cap, the safety tape should be maintained in place by the fingers of the hand in case it should unwind and pull out the safety bolt. Owing to the weight of this grenade limiting the distance it can be thrown, time must be allowed whilst it is in flight for the tape to unwind to withdraw the safety bolt; it is, therefore, advisable to throw well up into the air. The grenade should be thrown in a way most comfortable to the thrower, but it is recommended it be thrown by laying it along the forearm,

✠ " Never mind about the tape, it won't come undone ! " ✠

with the mechanism holder in the hand, at the same time maintaining a hold with the fingers on the safety tape. The grenade should be thrown with an overarm bowling action as used when throwing the No. 36 M. As soon as it has left the thrower's hand he MUST immediately take adequate cover, owing to the blast from this grenade being unusually heavy and quite lethal at a much greater distance than it can be thrown. Should the objective at which it is aimed be on softish ground it is advisable to throw the grenade high into the air to make sure there is sufficient shock when it lands to make the striker work should the target be missed.

NOTES.

Great care must be taken to make certain the explosive filling of the grenade is not exposed to moisture. This filling is also highly inflammable; therefore, never allow the grenade, with its safety lid off, to be exposed to or even be near a naked flame, or anywhere within reach of any kind of sparks. Precautions should be taken when having grenades in the field, but not being used, to keep them as much under cover as possible. They are very sympathetic to small-arms fire, and have been known to explode when fire of this nature has been taking place near by.

✠ " They won't detonate there ! " ✠

THE No. 74 S.T. GRENADE (STICKY BOMB).

Action : Concentrated blast. **Fuse :** Time, 5 secs.

The S.T. is supplied for service use packed in a metal case holding five grenades with five handles, whilst the detonator assemblies are supplied separately, five in a tube made of cardboard. One of these tubes should be fitted into the spring clips on the underside of the lid of the box. These grenades weigh approximately 2¼ lbs. each. The outer protective metal casing is coloured khaki, whilst the handle is black bakelite holding a No. 36 M. type striker, spring and safety pin. The No. 74 S.T. was designed for use against A.F.V's. Due to the nature of its special construction and the explosive used, it has the added advantage of sticking to its target as long as the target is not a wet, muddy, dirty, oily or steep, sloping surface. The No. 74 Grenade is most suitable for use at positions of ambush or in town fighting, for dropping from various parts of buildings on to AF.V's or other vehicles; can be useful at road blocks. The best results are obtained when it is used in the nature of a mobile demolition charge, placed in position by hand on the most vulnerable and least protected points of A.F.V's, in loopholes, walls, doors or windows of pillboxes, etc. It is specially recommended for night patrols when attacks are being made on enemy oil dumps, petrol stores, explosive depots, vehicle parks, etc. For some forms of structural demolition excellent effects can be obtained by using two S.T.'s, one held in the left hand, with the pin still in, smashed against the object to be demolished. The other S.T., with the pin withdrawn, is held in the right hand. Lay this (the right-hand grenade) on the already placed first grenade, release the lever. Take cover. Sympathetic detonation will explode both grenades. This method of demolition is advised because, as has been mentioned before, these bakelite handles snap very easily; therefore, in smashing down the left-hand grenade, it is immaterial whether the handle breaks or not as the second is placed in position. Further, the use of two " 74's " usually ensures that the hole blown through an average brick wall is large enough for men to enter. Before handling or demonstrating, make certain the grenade is not primed.

DETAILS OF GRENADE. (See sketch 17).

The body of the " 74 " grenade consists of a spherical glass flask 5 inches in diameter filled with 1¼ lbs. of nitro-glycerine, the explosive result of which is concentrated forward with a high degree of penetration. To protect the sticky envelope and fragile body of the grenade before use, it is completely covered by a metal casing consisting of two half spheres which are hinged at their base, maintained in position round the neck of the flask by a pin or clip. The actual flask itself is coated with a sticky envelope consisting of stockinette covered with bird lime ; this enables the flask to adhere, in ideal circumstances, to the object which it is intended to destroy. In the neck of the glass flask is a tube to hold the detonator assembly ; prior to fitting this, the neck is closed by means of wooden and rubber washers maintained in place by a screw cap. A throwing handle is fixed to the

✠ " I think that's a dummy detonator ! " ✠

neck of the flask by means of a screw ring. This handle itself contains the striker spring and striker, held in place by a lever which fits flush with the side of the handle. This in turn is held safely in position by means of a safety pin, the safety pin having a label affixed to it on which is marked, " Danger. Do not remove this pin until ready to throw grenade." Before use a striker test should be undertaken, similar to that given for the " 36 " M. Grenade. The actual detonator assembly is made up of a percussion cap, a detonator, a 5-sec. fuse, and a C.E. or composition exploding pellet.

HOW TO PRIME THE GRENADE.
Unscrew the neck screw cap which may have a piece of adhesive tape round it ; remove this, then remove the cap itself, take out the rubber and wooden washers, discard them. Next take a detonator assembly, removing the outer cardboard sleeve protecting the C.E. pellet ; insert the whole detonator assembly, with the pellet first into the tube. It should be noticed that the rubber rings fitted to the assembly will hold it quite firmly in position. Fit the handle of the grenade to the flask neck by screwing up the ring as tightly as possible. If this bakelite ring is loose the handle will almost certainly break when thrown. Sometimes it may be found this cannot be done ; should this be the case, try and assemble the grenade by using another spare handle and ring.

WARNING.
Make absolutely certain that the small knurled circular brass nut, holding the striker shaft in position in the lever head, s securely fastened. **Never** pull the pin until this precaution has been taken.

MECHANISM DETAILS.
When the safety pin is pulled out the striker is maintained in position so long as the user's hand firmly grips the lever, but on throwing or placing the grenade in position and releasing the hand, the pressure on the lever is naturally released, causing the lever to fly off. The powerful spring forces the striker down sharply on to and firing the percussion cap, which ignites the 5-sec. fuse, exploding the detonator, which in turn sets off the C.E. pellet which detonates the grenade.

HOW TO USE THE GRENADE.
Before use the outer casing, which may have a piece of adhesive tape round the actual joint, must be removed. This is done by pulling out the pin holding the two halves of the case together. NOTE VERY CAREFULLY : DO NOT pull the pin which has the label marked " DANGER " attached to it, as this will start the 5-sec. fuse working. When carrying out the above operation hold the grenade with the spherical portion hanging down ; this will allow the two halves of the outer metal

casing to fall off. Next pull out the safety pin, at the same time maintaining a firm grip on the lever, pressing it against the handle.
It will be found difficult to obtain any great degree of range with accuracy when throwing this type of grenade. The best results will be obtained by actually planting it on the object should circumstances permit. Make certain sufficient force is used to break the glass flask, then release the lever as sharply as possible. This will fire the cap and start the 5-sec. fuse burning, leaving you 4 seconds to get out of danger. If the grenade has stuck to a moving vehicle the explosion, of course, will be carried away from you. It has been estimated that if cover is taken about 10 yards away the user should be quite safe.

THE S.I.P. GRENADE (SELF-IGNITING PHORPHORUS). (See sketch 18).
Action : Incendiary and smoke. **Fuse :** None. Ignition by chemical action (when bottle broken).
This was designed as an incendiary grenade, consists of a ½-pint clear glass bottle containing yellow phosphorus, rubber latex, benzine and water. The grenade can be used either for throwing by hand or for projection from a Northover. There are two types which can be identified for their respective purposes as a red cap is fitted for hand-throwing only, whilst, if a green cap is fitted, the bottle is suitable either for hand-throwing or for projecting from the Northover. They are packed ready for use in plain wooden, flat, oblong boxes, marked with a green band at either end for Northover and a red band for hand-throwing, 24 in a box. The propellents for the green cap are packed in oblong cardboard boxes in which are cardboard tubes sometimes holding three propellants, but generally five to a tube—usually 30 propellants to the box. Make **certain** none of the bottles are

✠ " Tripe ! that's not a bottle of S.I.P. ! " ✠

cracked as the contents will cause dangerous burns if it comes in contact with flesh or clothing. Ignition is by chemical action, instantaneously when the bottle is smashed. The phosphorus, in contact with the air, ignites, setting fire to the rubber latex and benzine. These burning simultaneously cause a very considerable blaze of high temperature which is almost impossible to extinguish. The bottle and contents weigh approximately 1½ lbs.; when fired from the Northover can be projected from 75 to 150 yards. The range, when thrown by hand, is approximately 30 yards. Whilst burning, dense clouds of white smoke are generated, which is very useful as a smoke screen, and if broken on the front of a vehicle will, for a short time, make it impossible for the driver to see.

If using the S.I.P. for burning a house, practise will soon show how difficult it is to break these bottles in a room, particularly if it has been blitzed. About the only place where breakage is fairly certain is in the hearth or fireplace, which does not help much as the flames will probably be drawn up the chimney. The best method is to fasten a detonator with a short length of safety fuse to the bottle. Ignition of the fuse will explode the detonator, smashing the bottle and scattering its contents.

" 75 " and " 75A " GRENADE.

Action: Heavy blast. **Fuse**: Instantaneous detonation when crushed.

Generally known as **HAWKINS' GRENADE OR GRENADE MINE.** Designed for use against A.F.V's to immobilise them by damaging or destroying their tracks or under-carriage generally. The grenade itself is exploded by the weight of the vehicle passing over it, either by placing in the path of an approaching vehicle as a mine, or thrown in front from behind cover. When used as a mine it should be concealed just beneath the surface of the ground. A number of these grenades can be tied together about 3 feet apart, then pulled across in front of an approaching A.F.V. as opportunity occurs. In this form they become an effective road block. Do not string them closer together than 3 feet, as there is danger of sympathetic explosion taking place, unless, of course, this type of explosion is required; then fasten together less than 2 feet apart. This grenade has been proved a most effective, light, portable demolition charge, especially when operating against enemy rail communications. For this purpose use either a No. 8 Mark VII detonator or a No. 27 detonator with the necessary length of safety fuse. The grenade weighs approximately 2 lbs. 4 ozs. It can be thrown by hand about 20 to 30 yards.

Recognisable by its colour, which is dark buff, and its resemblance to a talcum powder tin. Its danger area is quite considerable particularly when, in bursting under its target, it causes pieces of the A.F.V. as well as the metal of the container to fly in all directions over a wide area. Under these conditions serious wounds can be caused up to 75 yards. With such a high blast effect it is more than likely that the metal displaced by the explosion may become lethal or create a great deal of damage inside the vehicle.

DETAILS. (See sketch 19).

There is no difference in appearance between the " 75 " and the " 75A " grenade, except that the latter is only approximately 80 per cent. as powerful as the former. It may be distinguished from the former by having the letter " A " stencilled on one side. The explosive content of the body is about 1½ lbs. ammonel and ¼ lb. of Victor powder. On the one side of the grenade are fitted two pockets which have slots in them intended to contain the detonator holders. These pockets can easily be closed, due to the flexible metal tabs. The actual contact point of the striker forms part of a plate, held above the detonator holders

✠ "That's O.K., sir, we've never had an accident on THIS range!" ✠

by means of two brackets, the striker itself being centrally located in the striker plate over the slots in the pockets. The cap at the body end MUST NOT be removed. It is actually cemented on to prevent opening, ensuring absolute freedom from any moisture. The igniter set consists of an igniter and detonator; two of these sets are for use with each grenade. The igniter is a tin-plate tube flattened at one end to close it; also recognised by being painted red. A rubber tube is rolled on to the igniter. The detonator is an aluminium tube open at one end, similar to those used in the other grenades mentioned before and should be treated as carefully as possible.

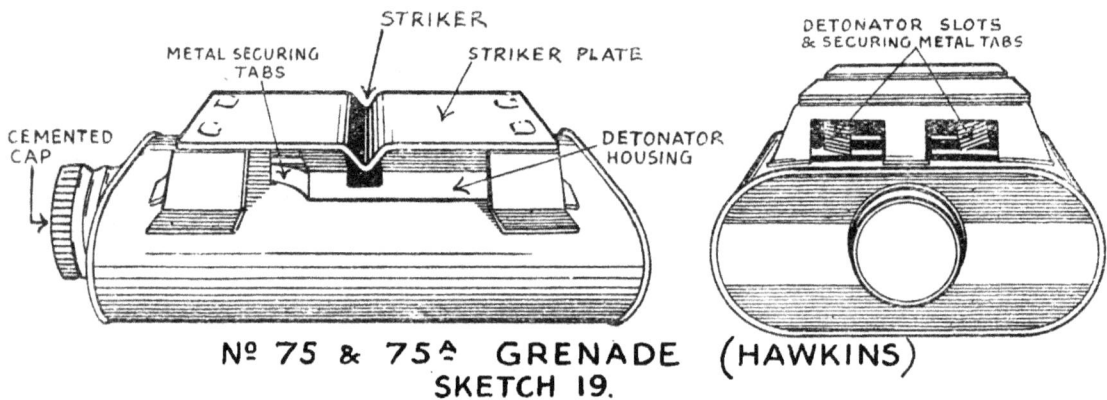

Nº 75 & 75A GRENADE (HAWKINS)
SKETCH 19.

MECHANICAL DETAILS.

The No. "75" and "75A" grenade has been very cleverly designed; the shape, generally recognised as that of a Talcum powder tin, was chosen for the "75" with the idea that no matter how the grenade is thrown it will always come to rest either with the striker plate underneath or on top. It will operate just as effectively in either position. What actually happens when the grenade is run over is as follows: Due to the weight of the vehicle the striker is forced down into the slots in the detonator holders, crushing the igniting tubes and breaking the glass capsules. This releases the acid in them; chemical action immediately takes place, causing a momentary flash, which sets off the detonators, so exploding the grenade. The Hawkins' has been designed to withstand an approximate weight of 2 cwt. before detonation commences.

PRIMING THE HAWKINS' GRENADE.

Firstly, take a detonator, fit the open end of the detonator into the open end of the igniter, allowing it to go home as far as possible without using any force. Then use the rubber tube on the detonator as a covering between the detonator and igniter; this is simply done by unrolling the rubber tube so as to cover the join—to assist as far as possible in making a water-tight joint. The igniter set should now be in position with the detonator end first, into each of the detonator holder pockets, inserting them through the holes in the striker plate bracket. Finally, bend over the metal tabs by means of which the detonator set will be firmly secured in position. The red painted part of the detonator units can now be seen in the detonator holder slots beneath the striker.

THROWING THE GRENADE.

These grenades may be thrown in any convenient manner, either projected overarm or lobbed underarm. It is suggested that a number should be strewn in the path of an on-coming vehicle, approximately one for every 3 or 4 feet of road width—the idea being that at the very least one should be detonated by an on-coming A.F.V. Should the grenade be thrown from the open without cover, the thrower must immediately throw himself flat—feet towards the grenade. In the event of some of the grenades not being detonated they can be recovered at a later opportunity and re-used. Care must be taken to see that grenades which have been damaged are not touched, as the slightest movement of these may give the final pressure required to start the igniter working, with certain fatal results. Should any damaged grenades be seen, the best thing to do is to note their position and ensure they are properly detonated as soon as possible. To disarm those not damaged for further use the igniting agent must be removed. This is effected by straightening the metal tabs individually, then carefully removing the two detonator assemblies, roll back the rubber tube so that it takes its original position on the igniter portion. Carefully slip out the detonator from the open end of the igniter tube, taking the usual care that must be taken with all detonators. Replace both in their respective containers.

THE No. 77 SMOKE GRENADE.

"BLINDS" (UNEXPLODED GRENADES). Destroying with "Demolition Set."

✠ " Go ahead, it's had plenty of time to go off ! " ✠

Occasionally when grenades are thrown or fired during practice they sometimes fail to explode; these are then known as "blinds." If this happens during training, under no circumstances can they be ignored as they are a source of constant danger. They must, as soon as possible, be dealt with in the correct manner, i.e., by using a "demolition set," consisting of a gun-cotton primer, a wooden rectifier, a detonator and a length of safety fuse, details of which are as follows :—(**See sketch 20**).

✠ " No demolition set ? Can't be helped. Carry on ! " ✠

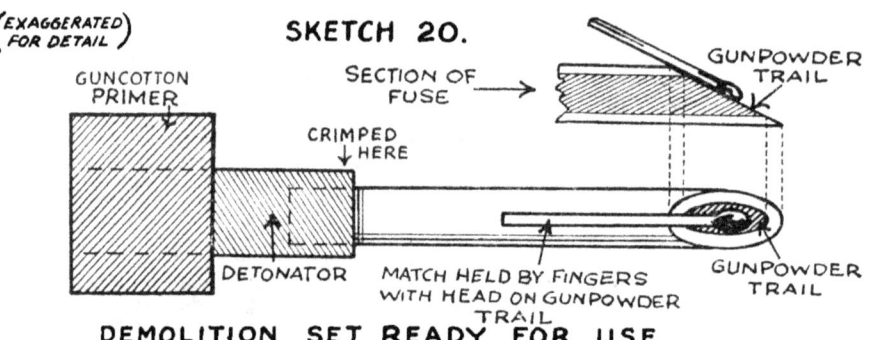

DEMOLITION SET READY FOR USE

FUSES.

Use **safety fuses only** for destroying " blinds "; the type usually supplied for this is known as the No. 11 Safety Fuse. It can be recognised as it is black, its outside being covered with waterproof tape. The centre of the fuse contains a gunpowder trail. It is normally issued in boxes containing 48 feet. Burns at the rate of 1 foot in 30 seconds or 1 inch in $2\frac{1}{2}$ seconds. These details should be found marked on the box. When unrolling the fuse do not strain it as there is a possibility of a kink or kinks occurring, breaking the continuity of the gunpowder trail and causing fuse failures. An urgent safety precaution is necessary before using, i.e., cut off a foot of fuse, ignite and time carefully. If this foot burns in less than 25 seconds **do not use** any more from this roll as it may have deteriorated or be the wrong kind. Failure to carry out this safety precaution may cause fatal accidents.

✠ " I think that piece of fuse will do ! " ✠

PRIMER.

The primers supplied for service use consist of gun-cotton; they are normally issued as circular 1-oz. pieces usually threaded on a piece of tape for easy handling, packed in a black metal tube.

DETONATORS.

Quite a number of kinds of detonators are in use amongst the various services. The type normally used for destruction or "blinds" is the No. 27 or the No. 8 Mark VII. This pattern of detonator is a small metal tube containing a quantity of extremely sensitive high explosive (fulminate of mercury). As in all detonators the greatest care **must** be taken as the slightest shock, scratch, crushing or even the heat of the hand will cause instantaneous explosion, which although probably not lethal can cause serious wounds.

DO NOT ALLOW FAMILIARITY WITH DETONATORS TO MAKE YOU CARELESS.

Always keep them covered as they are quickly affected by any moisture. The detonator is usually coloured red, labelled, and is supplied for service use in tins holding 25. For purposes of instruction the dummy detonator is supplied in tin—unpainted.

HOW TO ASSEMBLE A DEMOLITION SET.

Once satisfied that the fuse is of the correct type, cut off the amount required for use. This should be estimated by reckoning what length of time will be required to get to safe cover. Always be on the generous side when calculating the necessary length so as to give yourself plenty of margin. Allow about a couple of inches extra in length for the actual lighting of the fuse, check carefully to see the end of the fuse that is fitted into the detonator is cut quite clean and square. At the other end of the fuse bor a hole approximately 1 inch from the end through the fuse across its circumference. This can be done with the point of a sharp knife ; the hole should be of sufficient diameter to allow a match to pass through it so that the match can be pulled down until its head is projecting above the surface of the fuse—enough to be rubbed against a box to ignite. An alternative method is to cut the fuse at a steep angle to expose a good patch of powder ; hold the match head in this patch and rub the side of the match box to ignite the sulphur actually in contact with the powder.

Now take a piece of string, blade of grass or anything that will not scratch the sensitive explosive so as to measure the length of fuse required to enter the detonator **without** the end of the fuse pushing on the explosive. Leave ¼ inch clearance. Do not twist or turn the fuse while inserting into the open end of the detonator. Always hold the detonator by the **open** end. Insert the clean, square-cut end of the fuse into the detonator to the required length, then " crimp " or squeeze the detonator to the fuse,

✠" I always crimp detonators with my teeth ! "✠

using a pair of pliers, a knife blade or that part of a knife usually used for extracting stones from horses shoes, using the angle formed at the hinge when open and pressing the stone extractor downwards ; if these are not available, some form of mud may be used to hold the fuse in place to prevent it slipping out of the detonator between the high explosive and the cut end of the fuse.

The next operation is to take a gun-cotton primer, if necessary inserting the wooden rectifier in the central hole and twisting to ensure easy entry for the detonator, without the necessity of using any force to insert it. The detonator should be inserted sufficiently far so that its closed end is approximately flush with the other end of the primer. You now have a complete demolition set ready for use.

HOW TO USE THE DEMOLITION SET.

When it is required to destroy a "blind" the set should be placed in such a position that the primer is in contact with the "blind," but DO NOT move the grenade. Rub the match-box across the head of the match to ignite; this should start the gunpowder in the fuse burning; make certain of this before taking cover.

GERMAN GRENADES. Brief Summary.

THE ENEMY PROBABLY KNOW ABOUT YOUR GRENADES, SO SOME DETAILS ARE GIVEN OF THEIR BEST KNOWN TYPES.

The best known of the grenades issued to the modern German Army at present are the Egg and Stick Hand Grenades, Models 24 and P.H. 39. These are designed for offensive use but rely on blast as against fragmentation, as they are constructed with thin metal cases. In the case of both, but particularly the "stick" grenades, the blast can be lethal, but generally the result is severe shock and, or, anti-morale effects.

THE "EGG" GRENADE. (See sketch 21).

Grenades of this type were originally used during the 1914-1918 war and for recognition purposes are painted standard German Service dark grey-green colour, the outer thin casing can be recognised by the outside having an elevated thin flange round its middle. In the centre of the grenade a pocket is fitted which holds the standard No. 8 German Service pattern detonator and also contains a 5-sec. delay flash cap. This pocket extends, approximately, to a depth of two thirds of the actual grenade height.

HOW TO USE THE GRENADE.

To ignite the flash cap, there is a green knob approximately 5" in diameter at the top of the grenade. When the knob is pulled the flash cap is fired by a wire operating link. The flash cap is fitted to the grenade body by means of either a wing or square nut.

PRIMING THE GRENADE.

First check that the detonator pocket in the centre of the body is clean and free from burrs; then release by unscrewing the protective cap from the detonator end of the flash cap. Take a detonator and check carefully to see that its open end is absolutely clean. **This is essential.** Carefully adjust the detonator on to the detonator end of the flash cap by slipping it over it. Finally, screw in the complete fuse by means of the square nut or wing nut on to the grenade body.

All that is now required to use the grenade is to simply release the green knob by unscrewing it and pulling.

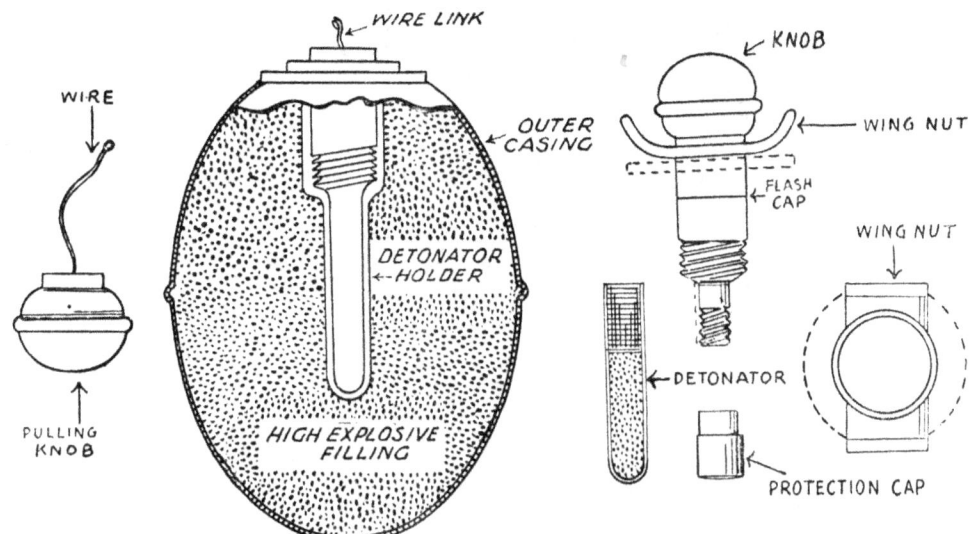

GERMAN EGG HAND GRENADE

SKETCH 21.

RECOGNITION OF GRENADE.

The "egg" shaped container is approximately 2″ in diameter at its thickest point, by 3″ in length. The grenade weighs approximately ¾-lb., and the standard fuse fitted to this grenade has a 5-sec. delay action. The High Explosive filling of this pattern of is very similar to gelignite.

It must be realised that a grenade of this weight can far out-range the British 36 M., further, the individual bomber can carry really large quantities, but whereas the 36 M can be fired from a Cup discharger, this grenade, so far as is known, can be hand-thrown only.

THE MODEL 24 STICK HAND GRENADE. (See sketch 22).

This grenade can be recognised by its similarity in appearance to the well known kitchen utensil the "potato masher"; in fact it was well known in the last war by this name. This type of grenade consists of a steel or iron head which contains High Explosive.

The explosive head itself is fitted to a wooden handle through the centre of which a double length of cord is run. One end of the cord is connected by a lead ball to the "friction" type Igniter Set, the other end of the cord is connected to a china bead which lies at the opposite end of the wooden handle in a small housing. This housing is covered by a screw cap to protect the china bead. When the grenade has been primed all that is necessary to make the grenade ready for use is to unscrew the cap at the opposite end of the wooden handle to which the explosive head is connected and simply pull on the china bead.

This has the effect of setting off the friction igniter set which, in turn, explodes the detonator.

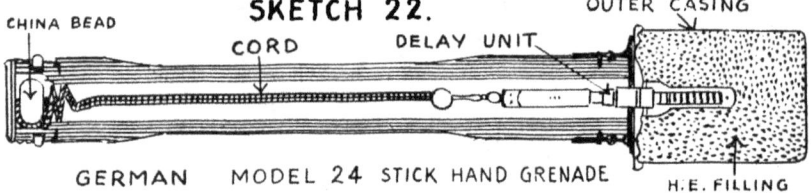

SKETCH 22.
GERMAN MODEL 24 STICK HAND GRENADE

PRIMING THE NO. 24 GRENADE.

Should grenades of this type be captured from the enemy, it will be found that they are usually without a detonator and to prime them it is necessary to release the wooden handle from the explosive head by unscrewing it.

When this is done it will be seen that the metal end of the delay fuse is just exposed in the bore of the handle. Carefully fit the detonator into this end of the fuse, finally, screwing the explosive head back on to the wooden handle, taking care that the threads do not get crossed. The grenade is now fully primed and ready for action. This grenade is fitted with 5-sec. delayed action fuse and for recognition purposes is approximately 1' 2" in total length and weighs just over 1¼-lbs., the explosive weighing approximately 6-oz.

With regard to range, these again can be thrown further than the British 36 M., the length of the handle helping considerably. It will be noted that 6-oz. of H.E. is quite a high proportion of explosive for a grenade of this weight.

THE MARK PH. 39 STICK HAND GRENADE. (See sketch 22).

This pattern of grenade is very similar to the No. 24 mentioned above and functions in exactly the same manner. The only difference in its operation is that when the cap protecting the china bead is unscrewed, the cap itself is used to fire the friction igniter set. This is done by giving the cap a sharp pull which automatically pulls the china bead beneath it and in turn pulls the cord and sets off the detonator. The difference in the outside appearance is that it is approximately 2" longer than Model 24 and about 1-oz. heavier. The weight of explosive is slightly more than the No. 24, being a fraction under ½-lb. This pattern of grenade has a faster delayed action fuse which operates in approximately 4½-secs. As far as is known the radius of effective danger when this grenade bursts is about 18 yards.

In spite of all the above grenades having a small danger area they have this advantage that they can be thrown considerably further distances than this area, making it unnecessary for the thrower to have immediate cover available.

The enemy has an unpleasant, but effective, habit of fastening the heads of either 6 P.H. 39's or 24's round a complete "stick" grenade. The explosion of the complete centre grenade causes sympathetic detonation, making a formidable and concentrated demolition charge which is particularly effective when used against A.F.V's, pillboxes, strong-points and in street-fighting as has been previously mentioned in using the British No. 73 and 74 S.T. grenades. The German method having the advantage of being a dual purpose grenade.

THE GERMAN HAND SMOKE GRENADE.

This grenade can be recognised by its likeness to the ordinary H.E. Stick grenade, but with the following difference: Instead of the normal grey-green H.E. explosive head being fitted, a smoke head is attached to the standard stick itself and the head is marked with a broken white band near its base. It also has stencilled on it the letters " Nb " in white.

AMERICAN GRENADES

Probably the most popular of the American grenades is the Mark II. This is very similar to the 36 M Grenade which is so well known. This grenade operates in exactly the same manner as the 36 M and has a similar serrated outer body, although it is more similar in shape to a large lemon than to the usual small pineapple shape with which we are so familiar. The H.E. content of this grenade is 2¼-oz. of Trojan Powder. This is a dry explosive which consists of 4 parts of purified starch saturated with a mixture of sulphuric and nitric acid and 6 parts of sodium and ammonium nitrates. The upper extremity of the grenade body has, screwed to it, what is known as the Bouchon Assembly. This consists of the Bouchon itself, the operating lever, and the sheet steel sealer. The Bouchon is a die-casting which is made up of a tube housing the standard Bickford safety fuse and leading to a fuliminated detonator which lies in the centre of the explosive charge. The Bouchon head remains outside the body and holds the priming cap, the striker and the firing spring. A safety pin, having a ring attached to it as in the 36 M, holds in place the operating lever which fits over the Bouchon head. For recognition purposes, the live grenades are painted grey. The practice grenades of this type are painted red. This grenade is used in exactly the same way as the 36 M, but is fitted with a 5-sec. fuse. The fragmentation danger radius of this grenade is approximately 100ft. Can be thrown for approximately 40 yards. **(See sketch 23).**

PATTERN MARK III HAND GRENADE. (See sketch 24)

This grenade consists of a cylindrical cardboard body at the top of which is fitted a die-cast cone, screw threaded, to receive the same standard Bouchon Assembly as used in the Mark II. This grenade operates in a similar manner to the Mark II, but due to the lack of a heavy metal casing it is used chiefly as an anti-morale bomb and while the blast is very concentrated, its actual effective danger radius is limited to about 15 yeads.

THE MARK II PHOSPHORUS HAND GRENADE.

This grenade consists of a barrel-shaped steel container approximately 2¼" in diameter and 3¼" high. The centre of which has a steel thimble screwed into it which in turn houses the Bouchon, its fuse and detonator, but keeping this separate from the phosphorus charge in the actual body of the container. Upon detonation, the phosphorus is released and when coming into contact with the air, burns and produces a very dense smoke. This grenade is particularly useful as a local smoke screen for hiding small movements. This pattern grenade has the same mechanism as the two previous grenades mentioned above and has the same 5-sec. fuse.

THE MARK V GAS GRENADE (Non Lethal Tear Gas). (See sketch 25).

This is an anti-personnel gas grenade, exactly similar in appearance and size to the above mentioned Mark II Phosphorous Grenade and the only mode of recognition that can be used to distinguish it from the Phosphorous Grenade is that near the bottom of the body there are two small flanges going completely round the body. This grenade has the same Bouchon fitting, holding

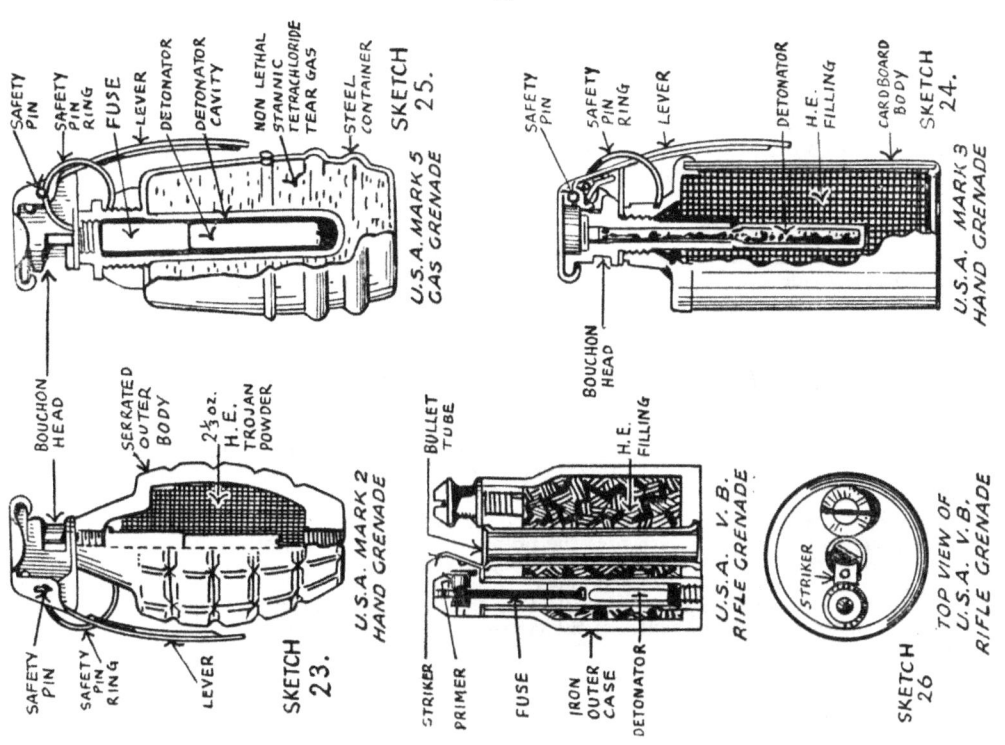

lever, detonator and fuse as in all the previously mentioned grenades and the actual gas that it contains is Stannic Tetrachloride, which is a tear producing gas. This pattern is particularly effective when dealing with rioting or clearing badly ventilated enemy strongholds.

THE INCENDIARY HAND GRENADE.

This is exactly similar in appearance and operates in the same manner as the above mentioned Mark II Phosphorous Hand Grenade and the Gas Hand Grenade, except that the body contains Thermite and solid oil.

THE RIFLE GRENADE. (See sketch 26).

This grenade is utilised for a similar purpose to our 36 M when fitted with a gas check and is fired from a Discharger in a similar manner to the British grenades when fired from an E.Y. Cup Discharger. This grenade is known as the VB Rifle Grenade. It is approximately 2½" in length and about 2" in diameter and is fired from the funnel shaped Discharger which is fitted to the American Service rifle. The body consists of a cylinder made of iron which is grooved on its inside so that considerable fragmentation effect takes place on explosion. The bottom of the grenade is flat and a hollow tube runs right through the centre of the grenade. The tube is to enable the bullet of the cartridge to pass through it when it is fired so that no special cartridge is necessary when fired from a rifle. As will be noted, this is contrary to the British practice of it being absolutely necessary to use a ballastite cartridge when firing the 36 or 68 from an E.Y. Cup Discharger fitted to the British Service rifle.

In the VB rifle grenade, a striker projects at an oblique angle over the fire end of the tube so that when the bullet passes through the tube it hits the striker which in turn fires the primer. The flash of the primer sets off the fuse which burns for 8 sconds and then in turn sets off the detonator which finally detonates the main explosive charge. This cycle of operations actually takes place whilst the grenade is in flight, because it begins to travel as soon as the bullet enters the central tube in the grenade. The expanding gases from the cartridge act as the propellent on the flat base of the grenade quite effectively as they strike this base before the bullet has passed through the centre of the grenade.

www.ingramcontent.com/pod-product-compliance
Lightning Source LLC
Chambersburg PA
CBHW081509040426
42446CB00017B/3441